Do You Hate
to Pay Insurance?

Free
Yourself

by
Rob McBride

First Edition
June 2019

RobMcBride
+58 414 328 6411
www.RobMcBride.net
rob.h.mcbride@gmail.com

McBride, Rob.
2050 The Big Change / Rob McBride.
MYBN 1962-0608-238-9-E

Do You Hate
to Pay Insurance?

Free
Yourself

by
Rob McBride

First Edition
June 2019

RobMcBride
+58 414 328 6411
www.RobMcBride.net
rob.h.mcbride@gmail.com

McBride, Rob.
2050 The Big Change / Rob McBride.
MYBN 1962-0608-238-9-E

I dedicate this book to my darling daughters Alicia and Chantalle, without you my life would be incomplete

Strategy

1) Inspire Yourself

2) Invest in Yourself

3) Insure Yourself

Table of Contents

Introduction

To free ourselves ourselves we need to achieve two primary objectives. The first is to prepare ourselves to handle financial obligations from an economic standpoint, and the second is to understand the emotional ups and downs that are inherent in the process.

While there are many definitions of freedom, I like this one:

"Freedom is the ability to do what you want, with whom you want, when you want, where ever you happen to be."

In my book, freedom does not depend on having a specific net worth, attaining a particular position at work, owning a business, or living in a particular part of the world. Being truly free means you live as you want to live most of the time. Of course, there are always exceptions, and even if you do free yourself, there will likely be things you don't want to do. Most important is to realize you almost always have a choice. For example, you may not want to renew your driver's license, but if you want to drive, there is no other choice, it's a requirement. As an alternative, you can choose not to drive, opting instead for public transportation, Ubers, or a chauffeur. We normally have some choice in most things we do.

True freedom means being able to take care of

yourself in the event of a crisis. What if the financial system as you know it were to completely collapse? Would you be able to take care of yourself? Recently countries like Zimbabwe and Venezuela have experienced hyper inflation which has eliminated the wealth of many and made the value of pensions paid negligible. What if you no longer had a job and the government ceased paying pensions and other social programs? What would you do?

While this certainly sounds like a good topic for a futuristic dystopian novel, anything is possible. In the United States of America, the pressure on the Social Security system is about to go through its biggest test ever, as Baby Boomers begin to retire. On another front, around the world central governments are increasing the money supply at record levels, without corresponding reserves to back them. This is an accident waiting to happen.

Health care is another topic which will continue to play big in the years to come. As people live longer, the costs to keep them alive also rise. How can we possibly plan today to handle the uncertainties of a lifetime?

This is precisely what this book is all about.

It is about dealing financially and emotionally with just about any emergency or situation that can come up. It is not enough to be able to handle the financial side of the equation, we must also deal with the emotional side, and this is perhaps the most difficult part. Not everyone has the temperament to have their own business and not everyone feels comfortable if they don't receive a paycheck every other Friday. Perhaps even more importantly, many people lack the discipline necessary to free themselves. It's every bit as much about our mentality, as it is about our capital base.

A financial net worth statement with several zeroes at the end of the first three numbers does not assure we will be able to handle the emotional side of the challenges we are likely to face. On the other hand, feeling we are free because we have the capacity to be independent and enterprising, doesn't necessarily make us so either.

Like a stool which balances best on three legs, we will examine three basic guidelines to free yourself. Each on its own will likely not stand the test of time, though it may help keep you on track. Together, the three of them form a strong base to keep you on track in the present, when the past threatens to envelope you and the uncertainty of the future paralyzes you.

Take a chance on you, beginning right now. Come with me to establish a financial and emotional base that can provide you with a lifetime of freedom.

Free yourself today...

It's as simple as 1, 2, 3!

1) Inspire Yourself

Each of the elements we are about to discuss is "Simple" in theory, but far from "Easy" in practice. Let me give you the definition I like best to differentiate these two similar words:

Golf is a very "simple" game. You hit the ball starting from the tee box, aiming for the green, and need only get the ball into the hole in a certain number of strokes (3, 4, or 5), depending on the "par" for the hole. For those who have ever played golf, they now that while the basic rules are quite "simple," it certainly is not "easy" to do.

Many things in life are quite similar. We often know what we are supposed to do, the difficult part is actually doing it and this is where most of us run into trouble. What I am about to explain is not rocket science. It's not some far fetched theory to get rich quick, magically changing your entire financial situation tomorrow. What I do offer is a simple, well designed path to free yourself from the dependence on others. To do this, you will need a great deal of inner motivation to stick with the plan when you run into obstacles, which surely will come. Resisting the temptation of the moment, in order to build a base for the future, is fundamental.

All of the theories in the world fall by the wayside if we do not put them into action. This is certainly the case with this manual you now have before you. If you take what I say and implement it to a "T", I've no doubt you will be able to free yourself financially and emotionally.   To do this, however, you must resist temptation and stick to your guns. Assuming you are able to resist temptation and build a capital base, many will want a piece of what you create, so you need to keep to your strategy, even when it seems like you can't.

How do you inspire yourself to be motivated and to resist temptation?

Inspiring ourselves is very much an "inside job." For some of us, our greatest motivation is family, for others it is work, yet for others it is their faith in God. We each have something which causes us to get up and go when we are feeling down and out.   Resisting temptation is as much about our will-power as our brain-power.

The first thing you need to do is to determine what inspires you, if you don't already know what it is. What lights your fire and gets you going when you are down?   Without knowing what motivates you, it's practically impossible to get past "Go," so determine what it is that starts your engines and fires you up, even when you don't feel so great.

The second step we will focus on to inspire yourself is to live what you love. If you love to be around surfing and the ocean, then find something to do where you can make money being close to both of those things. If you love reading and books, perhaps work in a library or in a bookstore could be your thing.

In this section, we will focus on what you will do if all else fails. If everything in the world goes to hell in a hand basket, what would you do? How would you live? For the worst case scenario, the best we can do is to be prepared to generate income doing something we love.

Finally to inspire yourself, we will look at your daily routine and what you can do to make it work for you. We all tend to have routines, whether we think about them or not. We have a certain way of doing things, and of carrying out our day. What we put into our mind on a consistent basis has a powerful influence on our results. Creating a powerful routine is essential to inspire yourself and resist temptation when challenges threaten to bring you down.

a) Determine What Inspires You

Our experiences shape us, making each of us different. Some have grown up in the lap of luxury, while others have lived in poverty. Some have parents who were caring and nurturing, while others had parents who are harsh and over-bearing. There is, however, one thing we all have in common. Into this world we were born and from it one day we will go. Where we go, and how we go is still up for debate, but the one thing for certain is we have a finite time on Earth.

When we look at a tombstone, with the birth date and death date separated by a dash; we realize that small dash represents each minute, hour, and day of our lives. What we do with that time is of paramount importance. We cannot always do what we want in life, and things are not always rosy and cheery; but we do have a choice on how to spend much of our time, so we should be wise as to what we do with it.

Naturally there are some things that inspire you and others that don't. For some Formula One racing is the greatest thrill on the planet, for others it's looking for new species of birds somewhere deep in the middle of nowhere. Some are more inspired by things that move our body, and others by those that move our mind.

Think about what you like, and why you like it. Do you like playing competitive games, or do you prefer playing music or acting? Each of us has something which calls our attention. Follow your instinct and gut feeling. If you can't somehow make this area part of your calling or your profession, as we will discuss in the next section, you can keep it forefront in your daily activities, because it will motivate you and give you energy.

Learn more about what interests you, and incredibly, it becomes even more interesting than you originally imagined. Do you like bonsai trees and gardening? If so, find out about events in the area where they discuss the craft and get to know others who are interested in the same things. As an added bonus you may end up with a life-long friend or a soul-mate, you never know.

Life is dynamic. The more we find out about a

particular subject, the more we find there is to know. One thought leads to another, and then another. When we are around what we love, we shine and are at our best. We stand a little taller, walk a little faster, and are more enthusiastic in our demeanor.

Do you know what inspires you?

If not, find something that does. It could be the most important thing you do.

b) Live What You Love

To free yourself, perhaps the most important step emotionally is to love what you do and to be able to make money at it. As a financial consultant, I told people how to invest their money to maximize their returns, and while this is important for financial freedom, no amount of money can replace your ability to make money right now, right here, today.

Perhaps none of us will ever have to face an apocalypse where the financial system collapses, or where pensions and subsidies become a thing of the past. What would happen if your capital base was wiped out? Could you begin again?

I'm not asking if you would like to begin again, I don't think any one would be so silly as to want to start over from zero, but many have come back time and again after serious financial and emotional difficulty.

History proves a person can make and lose several fortunes in a lifetime.

We tend to put a lot of emphasis on going to the university and being a professional. While a broad educational background may increase our overall knowledge of the world, it doesn't necessarily prepare us to go out into the world to make money.

A professional salesperson can easily get a job selling any one of many needed items in times of crisis. A beautician can still help his or her clients look their best, even in the toughest of circumstance. Policeman can continue to protect and serve, while firemen can put out fires. We will gladly pay these people for what they do, regardless of the situation.

As long as we have a way to generate cash flow, we will be fine tomorrow. We can be dropped in Timbuktu with the clothes on our back and as long as long as if we have a trade, profession, or some other way to earn money, then we have the ability come out on top.

When we link what we love with making money, then we automatically are bumped into the bonus round of life. If not, we may have to work at something to make a living, enabling us to do what we love. There are, after all, twenty-four hours in a day, and even if we take eight of them to sleep and eight to work, that still leaves 8 hours a day to divide up as we see fit. Linking what we love with what we do to live is perhaps the best way to create long-lasting happiness.

When we live what we love, we are excited to get

out of bed in the morning. We have things to see, places to go, and people to do, or uh well... you know what I mean. We see life as a never-ending adventure where each day is new and interesting. Get paid for what you love to do, and you are your well on your way to free yourself financially and emotionally.

If you are not able to live what you love for now, don't give up hope. Life is constantly changing and virtually anything is possible. Focusing your time, energy, and effort towards those things you love to do is the best way to create new opportunities in those same areas. Shake the trees with the fruit you like the most and see what falls. You are likely to find what you need to live what you love.

As an added benefit, the amount of capital you need to be free is diminished since you are better prepared emotionally to handle difficult circumstance, though keep in mind that certain trades and professions have a limited time we can effectively do them. Make sure you have a way to make money when your body begins to give out, even if it's in a teaching or advisory capacity, so that in a crunch, you always have a way to make money should you need it.

c) Create Your Routine

We all have routines we follow. Monday through Friday, we tend to get up at pretty much the same time, and in the same way. Some of us rise naturally with the first sounds of the new day, while others wake brusquely with the aid of an electronic rooster.

As we first open our eyes in the morning, our thoughts tend to be very similar from day to day. We often don't think twice about them. As we wake up, we may automatically turn on the radio, or the television. We usually spend about the same time in the bathroom and follow a similar procedure daily as we get dressed, get going, and get ready to go. We tend to eat something similar and do the same things before heading out the door.

For some people this is a very relaxed procedure, taking several hours. For others, if they are pressed for time, they can be up and out the door in less than ten minutes. We all spend our first hours of the day a little differently.

As we go to school, work, or our chosen activity for the day, we generally see the same people, take the same modes of transportation, and frequent the same places. We each create our own little bubble of activity doing something, before going back home again, after our mission is finished for the day.

Our evenings also are comprised of similar routines day after day. Saturdays and Sundays are often different, but they too take on their own particularity, with similar routines from one week to the next.

Some of the things we do empower us, others do not. When we stop and take a close look at how we spend our time, we often find there are several areas where we can make better use of our resources. Let's look at an example:

Let's suppose you turn on the radio or television to watch the news the very first thing in the morning. Why do you do it? Well, perhaps for several reasons. Among them may be that you feel it is important to know what is happening in the world, and maybe it is simply because it is what you have always done, without really thinking about it. Maybe it hasn't occurred to you to do anything different.

If it weren't for the incredibly negative nature of much of the news we hear, perhaps it wouldn't be such a bad idea to start the day finding out what's happening around the world. The reality is that the news we usually hear fills our first thoughts in the morning with images and sounds of robbery, rape, and murder; before going on to relate stories of genocide, war, and poverty.

I'm not saying these things don't exist and that we should turn a blind eye to what's happening around us, but rather to choose how, where, and when we get our information. When something important happens in the world, we tend to find out rather quickly. If the news and the media somehow ties into what you love to do, then by all means watch it, and do what you have to do; but don't let the negative nature of it take you down, as it so often can.

Ultimately you have control of what you put into your mind. In the morning you can awake to the soft sounds of a jungle, or the roar of the ocean, allowing your thoughts to dominate your environment, rather than vice-versa. Granted, we don't all wake up alone, or have the luxury of creating the ambient noise where we live, but by and large, we are in control of what we do

Rob McBride

throughout the day.

Here are some things we can do to empower our routines:

- Exercise

- Listen to music

- Read novels, inspirational writing, and/or poetry

- Meditate and listen to your environment with all of its sounds

- Take a walk in nature

- Listen to a Podcast regarding a hobby

- Watch videos specific to our profession or interests

Intuitively, we know we can do all these things, but often do not because we are used to doing something else. Turning on the radio, or hitting the power button on the remote control doesn't take much effort. Getting off our ass and doing something worthwhile takes more energy and effort!

We are generally pretty clear about what we "should" be doing, but don't always "do" it. Why is this?

There are many reasons. Temptation, laziness,

and conformity are the first three that come to mind.

Saving money is difficult because there is entirely too much temptation to spend it. This is likely the biggest challenge for people who want to build a capital base. In order to pay yourself 10% on an ongoing basis, you will have to say no to other things. If you are not able to resist temptation, concentrate on doing something you love to make money and live for the moment, because the financial part will probably not happen. We are tempted to spend our money thousands of times a day, if you cannot resist temptation, you will not be able to do as well building a capital base, plain and simple.

Being lazy is often much easier that getting up and doing something. Let's face it, taking a nice long nap in the middle of the day because your tired feels wonderful. The fact of the matter is that if you get off your ass and into the world today, it will help you to put it wherever you want tomorrow. But this is nothing new. Virtually nothing is achieved without some kind of sacrifice. You will never make it to second base unless step off of first.

Doing "what we have always done," somehow feels right. Why would we want to rock the boat and do something different? The answer is simple. If you do not have a solid base to inspire yourself through difficulty, emotional pressures will inhibit you from freeing yourself and reaching your objective. You must have something which makes you want to get up and go rather than staying down and out for the count.

People will tell you:

- "Being debt-free is silly. After all, what kind of a tax break do you get if you don't pay mortgage interest?"

- "Think of the money you are leaving on the table if there is a sharp rise in the value of real estate, don't be stupid."

- "No one owns their own home these days, leverage your home to your benefit and buy that boat you have always wanted."

- "All the neighbors have new cars, isn't it time we get one?"

These and many other arguments will be our nemesis as we do our best to stick to our guns. We need a powerful way to get back on track when others try to knock us off. The best way I have found is to make our routines as empowering as possible.

What should your routines be and when should you do them?

It depends on you. If you are a morning person, I would suggest your daily dose of motivation be shortly after you wake up. If you are more of an afternoon or night person, wait until then to inspire yourself, but make sure you do it DAILY.

While there are many different ways to inspire ourselves, my daily deed starts with a cup of coffee at about 6:00 AM. While the rest of the country listens to the National Anthem on the radio here in Venezuela, I begin reciting a series of my favorite quotes. Starting with the Seeds of Success from Og Mandino, from his excellent book MISSION: SUCCESS, and ending with WHAT A WONDERFUL WORLD by Louis Armstrong. Reciting these words and reflecting on them as I consider my challenges for the day has become part of my routine.

I tend to find solutions to my problems, and better understand how I will face the day. Reciting the words non-stop takes a little less than 30 minutes. In actuality, often it takes an hour or more each day, as I repeat the words while doing my morning tasks. The process is magical to get my attitude right, particularly when it's gone a little South.

You can find a sampling of the words I repeat daily in the appendix. Adopt my words, or better yet, find your own! When you do, read them daily. I highly encourage you to memorize them, that way you don't even need to read them. It's actually easier than you think. Suppose you want to memorize a paragraph of text. Start today with the first few words. Begin tomorrow with what you remember from today. Pretty soon you will have the first sentence, then the second, and then the entire paragraph.

Have the words right at the tip of your tongue whenever you should need them. The positive effect of memorization and repetition has been used with religion with great success for years. We too can benefit from the same dynamic, using words which empower and inspire us. They could come from a poem, perhaps a speech you heard. The lyrics in songs are also often a great source of inspiration.

If you like, record the words in your own voice and make them easily accessible to hear when you are ready. There are also many excellent audios and videos that can empower our thoughts daily. Or, if you prefer, listen to music which enlightens you, taking advantage of the time to stretch and do some exercise. Perhaps putting on your favorite music and dancing naked is your thing, we all have something different that motivates us and not even the sky is the limit when we want to inspire ourselves.

Find what turns you on, and then keep pushing the button day after day. Here is an idea for you. Find a nice box and collect things in it that make you feel good. It could be a picture, a letter, a stone, a seashell, or just about anything that connects you with a positive emotion. Whenever you are feeling down, get out the box and look through it. You are surely to feel better after taking a look.

Perhaps your most difficult task in this phase is to be able to resist the temptation to spend more money than you earn, saving nothing and going into a wicked debt spiral. In today's society, this is the way many go with so many opportunities to spend our money. I'm not against spending what you earn, just make sure you pay yourself first, at the get go, and then enjoy the rest. After all, it is your money and there may be no tomorrow.

Do whatever it takes to inspire yourself to greatness. Use positive routines to keep your mind and occupied, helping you to free yourself from the forces of temptation which are bound to compete with for your money. Use these same routines to get back on track, when you feel yourself getting side-tracked.

2) Invest in Yourself

Another of the pillars to free yourself is to have a capital base providing you with the financial ability to handle life's challenges and live as you desire.

To understand investing in yourself, always keep one thing in mind. For a business, there is one primary goal: they need to make a profit. A company that doesn't make money will soon be out of business, and that isn't good for anyone. This is the way of the world. The strong survive and the weak are slaughtered. We can use this information to our benefit, but before we do, we need to have some capital to work with, and this is where most people fall short. As the old saying goes:

"People don't plan to fail, they fail to plan."

Most people who live and die in the world live hand to mouth for the great majority of their lives, simply because they don't know any better. They don't know there is an alternative.

Frequently people will tell me, "I will start saving money when I make more money." That's hogwash. If you don't save money when you don't make much, you are not likely do so when you make more.

In my working lifetime, I have made what I consider to be a lot of money, and not so much money. Miraculously, what comes in goes out. When we have more income, we increase our expenditures; when we have less, we decrease them, but somehow we always spend the money.

The process of making and spending money is similar to placing sand in the top of a funnel and watching it come out at the bottom. While the whole process to me is somehow magical, what is for certain is that it generally takes longer to put the money in the top than it takes for it to go out from the bottom

Mostly the sand we put in usually goes in little by little, while it seems to go out much quicker. The sand leaking out of the bottom depends on our expenditures. If we spend more than we make, the top part is always empty. This is the case for many of the people around the world.

Our goal here is to build a surplus in the top part of the funnel, while controlling the amount that leaks from the bottom. There is one very simple way to do just this. We need only spend less than we earn. Easier said than done, right? As tends to be the case with so many things, it is much easier in theory than to do in practice. Here we see once again where giving into temptation can easily turn us upside down. If we spend more than we make, eventually we will run into problems, period.

How do you build capital in the top part of your financial funnel?

Simple, you pay yourself first.

Take 10% of every dollar you earn and transfer it to a separate account in your name, before you pay anybody else. If you get paid $10, you transfer a $1. If you get paid $500, you transfer $50, and so on...

Sounds easy, right?

It's not... I would say it's very "Simple" but far from being "Easy."

With so many temptations at hand, we always have something we can spend our money on. These days, we don't even need the money. With credit we can spend more money than we have in a heartbeat. As we spend more and pay more, our credit rating goes up, allowing us to get more in debt. We find ourselves in a world where many things seem to cost only $40 or $50 a month, yet somehow all these small costs add up to be thousands of dollars a month. Like a mule running after a carrot before him, month after month we run, just to stay even.

Another way to think of our financial health is to compare it to the scales of justice. If you keep putting more expenses on one side, without compensating the other with income, you will eventually get upside down, and in today's world, it's so very easy to get there. If you have ever gone through bankruptcy, you know just how easy it is to get in trouble with the credit game.

Instead, tip the scales to your side, by taking 10% of every payment you receive from now on, and setting it aside. Little by little the extra weight on the asset side of your scales will enable you to free yourself financially.

I know what you're probably thinking, "Yeah, right! I'm already in debt up to my eyeballs and can barely pay what I have now, so how am I going to save 10%?"

The answer is simple, you just do it, and don't tell

anyone. We are talking here about your financial stability for the rest of your life. Why would you possibly put the electric bill, the telephone bill, the rent, or any other payment above your future? It makes no sense, yet we have been so conditioned to pay our bills before investing in ourselves, that we don't even consider the possibility of saving money. We get caught up in the day to day, and before we know it, we have too much month at the end of the money. Has this ever happened to you? Then taxes come and if we haven't taken proper measures, we are nailed once again to the wall, putting us even deeper into debt. It's a vicious cycle and trust me, you don't want to go there.

Instead, whenever you get ANY KIND of payment, you automatically make a transfer to your separate account for 10%. If it's a bigger payment than you normally get, consider giving yourself a bonus. Go ahead, be generous, you deserve it!

There will be times when emergencies will come up, and unexpected things will happen, this is a part of life. Just make sure you keep your eye on the ball in terms of priorities in order to free yourself from financial slavery.

I realize that right now having more in your bank account than the check you just got paid may seem an utter impossibility, but believe me, it's not. It's simply a matter of common sense and discipline. If you pay yourself first, and leave that money intact, your account balance will constantly be rising. This money is not for taxes, or a new computer, or the latest potato peeler you just saw on television. It's to enable you to free yourself in the future, so don't screw it up.

If you get a check for $261.45, transfer $27. Why would you cheat yourself and round the numbers down? Round up whenever possible. Why not be a really big spender and give yourself $30?

If you get an unexpected payment for $1,250, 10% is $125. Why not consider doubling your transfer to yourself by giving yourself $250? You still have $1,000 left over, and you will have saved 20%, instead of your usual 10%. Now here comes the best part of investing in yourself first. After you pay yourself at least 10% right off the top, go and spend the rest. Have a ball, it's your money. You don't even need to skimp or be stingy. Spend it all, be happy in knowing you are well on your way to paving your financial freedom, while at the same time living in the present!

Don't think too much about it, just do it. The results you see over time will be phenomenal. If you are earning $50,000 a year, you should be saving a minimum of $5,000 a year. It may not sound like much, but it's a start.

Initially a bank savings account is more than sufficient for your needs. It doesn't pay much interest, but the money will be there when you need it. Don't get enticed into get rich schemes early on, don't play the stock market, and please don't lend it to your brother-in-law; unless it's a life or death situation and you have no other choice.

By the way. If you do have a life or death situation, use the money, that is what it's there for, but don't kid yourself into spending the money for anything other than creating your ability to free yourself.

In this section we will start by creating an emergency fund. Once that is well in place, we will talk about risk tolerance and then delve into many of the options available for investing your hard-earned money. I will then discuss the purchase of real estate and close by elaborating a plan to become debt free.

* As a side note for anyone reading this who lives in a hyper-inflationary environment, like Venezuela. Please do NOT invest money in your local currency, spend it as fast as you can. Instead, with any money you earn, invest the 10% you save into something that is readily marketable. It could be anything from hard currency, gold, or motor oil. Find something that is easy to store, will hold its value in foreign currency and won't spoil. In a highly inflationary environment, you don't want to have money in the bank.

a) Create an Emergency Fund

The most challenging part of the process will be to get going. The first thing to do with the 10% you pay yourself is to create an emergency fund. The amount you accumulate depends on your confidence regarding your ability to produce money if you lose your job. I would suggest putting aside 3 to 6 months of emergency funds in this separate savings account before you ever even think about investing in anything other than a savings account. This bank product is far from sexy, and has no bells or whistles, but it is an essential part of your over all strategy.

Figure out your monthly expenses right now, all in, how much do you spend? Multiply this number by three or by six. This will be your initial goal on your way to financial freedom and insuring yourself. If you currently have $3,000 in total monthly expenses, your initial goal is to put from $9,000 to $18,000 into a SEPARATE savings account in your bank. Make sure it is separate from the account from which you make and receive payments. It's very important you put this money into a different account so you won't be tempted to draw on it in a moment of weakness, giving into temptation.

A savings account in a bank may seem very unsophisticated, but having money at hand in a moments notice, gives us tremendous peace of mind. Banks have been the traditional place to do this and they provide a service, for this privilege we give them our money to keep it for us. Always remember, it's your money, not theirs. That doesn't keep them from using it, but they do provide a function. You should have a very minimum of two accounts to start out with, a checking account for your day to day needs, and a savings account for the money you are about to save.

You may not think it possible. Right now you might be in debt up to your eyeballs, as I've said before, but you can begin today, I promise you. At first you can't imagine how it can possibly work, but it does.

When you have three to six months of your monthly expenses set aside, you know you can at least handle a situation where you may need to go without income temporarily. This will enable you to get back on your feet again without undue heartache and stress.

When you have money set aside to handle a major emergency, you walk a little taller and feel a lot more confident in your ability to handle the nuisances of life, which all seem somehow to cost money. When you have a readily available cushion to handle life's unexpected events, you sleep much better at night. Getting there is not easy, and it will likely take you a few years, but what the heck, we'll get there one way or the other, sooner or later. As an added benefit, when you see your stash of cash growing, it will give you a warm fuzzy feeling inside.

With an emergency fund firmly under your belt, you're ready to take off your "training wheels," and start riding with the big boys and girls.

b) Establish your Risk Tolerance

Investing is much like going to Las Vegas. Some could never imagine going there to gamble, preferring instead to stay home and watch Netflix, or catch up on the local news. Others would be there every day of the year, if they didn't have to work. The dynamics of investing in yourself has many similarities with the dynamics of gambling. What I aim to do is to stack the deck in your favor, so that you walk out a winner rather than a loser.

When people go to Las Vegas, most expect to have some laughs and good fun, but those who gamble, they also expect they will likely lose some some money. Others may go there for the entertainment, but choose not to gamble.

For those who choose to play all the games available to try you luck, they can have the time of their lives. Throwing money around in chips which somehow seem unreal can be a lot of fun. Watching your money grow as your luck is good is thrilling. Watching it go away just as quickly can be heartbreaking.

Most of us hate to lose money and yet many know from experience that is often what happens when you gamble. Most people don't go to Las Vegas to make money, rather to go with the flow and have a good time. By the way, those who walk away winners in gambling, and in life, do one thing very well. They walk away when they are ahead.

In Las Vegas, we know the house always wins. All we need to do is look around at the neon lights, the glass, the glitter, and the gold to see this to be true. Still we gamble, because it's great fun for many. This is one of the funnest and most interesting places in the world, but have no doubt, odds are we will leave more cash in the casinos than we take out. It's planned this way, we all know the rules and accept them. Life is quite similar.

For those who don't like to gamble at all, they can stick to bank savings accounts and certificates of deposit. Others can can step up to a slot machine or belly up to the tables to invest in a wide variety of stocks, bonds, and other investments.

Our most important goal here is to assure our risk tolerance is properly represented by the investments we choose. The investment is not the right one unless it fits our mentality. The investments with the most upside potential also usually have the most volatility. If a lot of risk might might give you a heart attack, then it may not be worth the stress. Choose your investments carefully to keep your emotional health as well as your financial health.

Each place you can invest your hard-earned money has a degree of risk and a possible return. We need to carefully consider the risk we are willing to take and then let this guiding light determine our investments, rather than getting all excited about the latest greatest company your cousin Louie told you about. This is a rule of thumb regarding risk and return:

Higher returns are most often accompanied with higher risk and greater volatility.

In Las Vegas, the more risk you are willing to take, the more you can win, or lose. This is the same with investments. If you are being offered a higher rate of return on your money, there will likely be higher risk associated with it, even if it is being promoted by your favorite celebrity, and perhaps more likely as a result of the endorsement. In Las Vegas, the house does surprisingly well with only a slight edge with only a slight edge on many of its most popular games. With regards to investment opportunities, the possibilities of gain and loss are often much greater.

It's no surprise that when you have money, everyone becomes your friend. This includes anybody with a hair-brained idea to make more money. The catch is generally that they need your money to do it. Friends you didn't even know you had appear out of no where, and you are kinda like a rock star when people know you have some cash, but beware, this can lead to pitfalls in your financial health.

Better yet, don't tell anyone what you are doing. Instead, be a legend in your own mind, and simply stick to your strategy. Keep your head down, ass up, and watch your backside, as you pack away your 10% each time you get paid, little by little.

Since there are so many options in this area, I will start with a straightforward strategy that should work most of the time, but as is the case with many things, anything can happen. As is the case in Las Vegas, we can gain or lose a lot in a short period of time if we aren't careful.

Are you feeling lucky?

Let's go!

Rob McBride

i) Stock Market

Together with real estate, I believe a wise investment in stocks to be the best opportunity for sustained growth over time to build your capital base. The road can be very bumpy, and believe me, losing 10% of your hard-earned capital doesn't feel the same as gaining 10%. Losing $100 in Vegas on a night on the town is a lot different from losing $10,000 on the first $100,000 that you are GOING to have as a part of your base — Nudge, nudge, hint, hint... I'm talking to you!— when you follow this simple plan.

As we just talked about in our discussion about risk, if you don't like to lose money in Vegas, then you probably won't want to lose it on an investment. I certainly felt that way initially. Then I realized that not adventuring into investments is much like going to Las Vegas and not betting anything at all. It probably takes away a lot of the fun and the excitement.

In addition, when we begin to understand that the banks and the insurance companies rely heavily on these same investments, we begin to better understand the relationship between risk and reward.

As I have already mentioned, those who get out of Vegas and life as winners have one thing in common. They all stop when they are ahead. You should do the same with your money and your investments. Don't get greedy, stop when you are ahead and move on.

The stock market may seem like this huge unknown mass of companies that make little sense. But when we understand that behind the companies, the stock prices, and hoopla, there are boards of directors and employees all directed at doing one thing. They all want to make more money. The head honcho wants the salespeople to sell more. The salespeople want operations to deliver their product faster. They all want better benefits and working conditions.

Economic conditions generally affect most companies positively or negatively at the same time, while fraud or other illicit activity can cause the price of a single stock to skyrocket or plummet dramatically in a single day. Yet they all continue with their primary mission, which is to make money. Each person who works at the company strives in some way to cut costs and increase revenues, in some way or another.

Over time investments in stocks have done a pretty good on average. This is the tricky part, since intrinsically, "average" includes a lot of ups and downs along the way. On the whole the prices of most stocks have gone up over the long-term, but in the short-term, it's anyone's guess where they will go. This is where things can start to seem confusing.

In order to make sense of all these different options, there are many companies willing to give you advice on what to do with your money. Make no mistake about it, the advice you get has a fee associated to it in some way. You may not have ever see it, and it may never show up on your statement, but somebody has to keep the water running and turn on the electricity in the multi-million dollar buildings they occupy.

I'm convinced the reason most people would choose to use a financial advisor, over making his or her own investment decisions, is to be able to blame someone if something goes wrong. Something similar happens with insurance, as we transfer the risk to the insurance company; but more on this later.

If you go to a financial consultant, they will give you advice, and likely it will pretty good advice, but expect to pay a price for it. He or she also has a family to feed.

If you are more adventurous, open a brokerage account, get on-line access, and within several minutes you will probably be ready to trade in the stock market for a few dollars per transaction.

The two investments I like best in terms of risk and reward replicate two well known indexes. Their symbols are:

1) DIA - SPDR® Dow Jones Industrial Average

2) QQQ - Invesco NASDAQ Trust

Their overall expense ratios are among the lowest available, and perhaps the best part about these two investments is that you need not pay too much attention to them, and what's more, you probably shouldn't if you know what's good for you.

With an emergency set aside, I suggest this is

where your additional money should go to maximize returns. This money can later be used to purchase a house, start a business, or for any other purpose, but for now it's your long-term money. As such, you need to put it to work for you in the capital markets.

Since inception, in 1998, DIA, which mirrors the Dow Jones Industrial Average, has given an average annualized return of 8.1%, while since 1999, QQQ, which mirrors the Nasdaq 1000, has given 7.1%. These numbers may not seem very inviting, but they are quite a bit more than what has been available at a bank over the same period of time.

The interesting part is how we arrive at these returns on a year by year basis. It looks much like a roller coaster.

Check out the returns on the following page since the inception of each of these investments:

Year	DIA	QQQ
1999	25.84%	--
2000	-7.30%	-36.11%
2001	-6.54%	-33.34%
2002	-16.32%	-37.37%
2003	25.22%	49.61%
2004	2.81%	9.49%
2005	-0.52%	1.23%
2006	16.33%	6.81%
2007	6.54%	18.67%
2008	-33.97%	-41.94%
2009	18.91%	53.83%
2010	11.11%	19.04%
2011	5.38%	2.52%
2012	7.16%	16.66%
2013	26.72%	35.05%
2014	7.50%	17.38%
2015	-2.19%	8.34%
2016	13.52%	5.92%
2017	25.25%	31.47%
2018	-5.73%	-0.96%

* http://www.1stock1.com/1stock1_2343.htm

* http://www.1stock1.com/1stock1_2312.htm

If you want to get your adrenaline going, and see how you will feel in the rough times, take a look at the first few years of this century, when these two funds were just getting started, and then again in the year 2008.

At first glance, this degree of volatility may be a deal breaker for you, and if so, that's fine. There is a huge emotional element involved with owning any kind of investment. If you do not feel comfortable with what you are doing, it doesn't matter how large the potential return, you are likely to bail out of the investment at the worst time. In actuality, when the market goes down, is when we should double down and put more, but it's difficult to do. Instead, we tend to get nervous, sell out, and then avoid stocks like the plague.

The stock market is not good or bad, it simply is what it is. Sometimes we win, and sometimes we lose, but the big difference is that here I believe we are the "house" and that over time we will come out on top, if we stick to our strategy.

Volatility can actually work to our advantage because of something called Dollar Cost Averaging. In layman's terms, this simply means that we put relatively constant amounts of money into an investment periodically over time. The way the math works out, our average cost will be less than the average price, regardless if we are in a rising or a falling price environment. The math has always amazed me. Obviously if the investment just goes down and never goes up, we still lose our money; but if and when it does come back up, we will benefit greatly by having purchased more stock at more favorable prices. Here's an example to show you how it works:

Date	Amount	Price	Shares	
January	$500	$100	5	
February	$500	$125	4	
March	$500	$150	3 1/3	
April	$500	$200	2 1/2	
May	$500	$175	2 6/7	
June	$500	$125	4	
July	$500	$75	6 2/3	
August	$500	$50	10	
September	$500	$25	20	
October	$500	$50	10	
November	$500	$75	6 2/3	
December	$500	$100	5	
Totals:	$6,000	$1,250	80	
	$1,250 / 12	$104	75	$6,000 / 80
		Avg. Price / Share	Avg. Cost / Share	

Granted, here I am showing extreme volatility to make a point. Think of the emotional roller coaster you might go on if a year was actually like this! Yet, if you stick to your guns, putting in your $500 per month as the price rises and falls, you end up benefiting in the end. Your average cost per share is $75, while the average price over that time is over $100. Don't ask me how it works, and don't take my word for it. I've worked the numbers many times and in many different ways. Our average cost ends up being less than the average price when prices increase or fall. Obviously, we will only make money if it goes up and certainly lose money if it goes down, but at least we will be happy in knowing we paid a bit less in the process.

Let's talk about losses. No one likes them, but keep in mind they are only paper losses, unless you sell, then they become very real. When is the right time to sell? Easy, when you have lost confidence in the company, investment, or strategy. If you invest, there will be times when market volatility will test your grit and resolve. There will be times you want to stray from your mission, don't. Keep putting your 10% away and stick to your guns.

Find other stocks you like. Look around you. Is there a particular company doing well with a new innovative idea? It could be the next Microsoft. Don't put all your money in any one particular investment, but perhaps take a shot and invest some of your capital in an new and upcoming company or idea. It could do very well, or you could lose it all.

Risk is relative, and yet always present. Even investments directly into U.S. Government backed securities have an element of risk, which we will discuss next. But realize risk and reward are generally opposite sides of the same coin. If there is a lot of risk on one side, there is generally a lot of potential on the other. Likewise, if there is a low return on one side, the risk is also likely to be lower on the other, but watch out! There are thousands of scam artists out there itching to take your hard earned money away from you, be careful!

Don't talk about what you have and what you do, unless its with a very trusted individual, and even then, be careful. Instead, do one simple thing that will make a huge difference in your life. Pay yourself first and invest in the capital markets after you have an emergency fund. How big of a difference can it make? Here are the numbers on several scenarios:

Monthly Savings	100 / month	250 / month	500 / month
10 yrs @ 0%	$12,000	$30,000	$60,000
10 yrs @ 7%	**$17,308**	**$44,485**	**$88,965**
20 yrs @ 0%	$24,000	$60,000	$120,000
20 yrs @ 7%	**$52,093**	**$138,432**	**$276,865**
30 yrs @ 0%	$36,000	$90,000	$180,000
30 yrs @ 7%	**$121,997**	**$336,861**	**$673,722**

Everything else being equal, you will always have more money if you save, than if you do not; but obviously you will have much more if you can earn a decent rate of interest on your money.

If you must be conservative, then be so, but also realize you may be leaving a lot of money on the table, as the examples above indicate. Choose wisely.

ii) Bonds

There seems to be quite a lot of talk a lot about bonds in the news, and while they can be a good investment for many reasons, they are primarily for those who want to take a more conservative view.

Nevertheless, beware as here too lurks danger.

In a nutshell, bonds are generally issued by companies and central governments to raise money. Those who purchase the bonds give their money in exchange for two things. The first is a specified interest rate; and the second, is the promise to have the money repaid at the end of a particular period of time.

Each of the companies, or governments, who issue the bonds has a different rating. Those with the best ratings pay the lowest interest rates, while those with the worst ratings pay the highest.

Does this sound familiar?

It should because it is exactly the same in the example with stocks we just discussed, only different...

In this case, there are several risks we have which are much more subtle.

1. If interest rates go up, the value of our investment goes down

2. If interest rates go down, certain bonds can be prepaid, requiring reinvestment of those funds at lower rates

3. If the lender goes bankrupt we will have to stand in line to get our money back

As you can see, there are several factors involved in choosing a portfolio of bonds. Many people enjoy picking and choosing their own bonds, from different issuers, with different ratings, and for different periods of time. One such strategy is a laddered approach where maturities are staggered at specific intervals to assure some money comes due periodically to provide for liquidity if needed.

Some bonds offer tax benefits for certain investors, and are called "tax-free" bonds. You can find thousands of financial consultants who will be happy to do the leg work for you and help you to choose a portfolio of bonds, though it certainly isn't their favorite thing to do, since it doesn't provide them or their company very much revenue.

A well chosen portfolio of bonds could be worthwhile for conservative investors who want to get a bit more interest than the banks provide. After all, this is type of investment often used by banks and insurance companies to invest their funds.

Even if you do hold the bonds to maturity to limit capital loss due to rising interest rates and carefully choose the issuers to avoid default, personally I don't think it's worth the hassle for the small incremental return over what we can earn in the bank, nor as much as we can get in stocks if we are savvy.

iii) Banks

We have to give banks their space in this phase of the process as well. They also have products available for our "long-term" money. The main product they offer is a Certificate of Deposit.

Very similar bond issued by a corporation or government, which we just discussed, the bank promises to pay a specified interest rate for a particular period of time. The interest rate is generally higher for longer deposits and typically rises as the amount deposited rises. If you need the money before the maturity date, the penalty is usually limited to lost interest, if the deposit is canceled early.

Though many people discount certificates of deposit, they do actually have a purpose, and they can even be used for the "shorter-term" money you have to boost your interest rates a bit.

As an example. As you are on your way to having six months of living expenses, the amount you save will add up to a considerable amount of cash in your account. Though the difference in interest rates between savings and certificates of deposit tends to be small, every little bit helps. The additional amount of interest never seemed so appealing to me, and I preferred instead to have funds completely liquid or invest it in something with greater upside potential. Notwithstanding, these investments can boost your returns slightly.

iv) Insurance Companies

Insurance companies offer products to protect us against risks we are not willing to assume and they also offer investment vehicles for our hard-earned money. I will address the risks they cover in the next section, but for now let's take a look at three products they offer as long-term savings vehicles.

You can invest in an annuity through insurance companies, whereby they will take your money from you as either a single premium (payment), or in several premiums. Your money then typically accrues with taxes on interest being tax deferred until you take it later on, presumably for retirement.

While the tax-deferred option on annuities is attractive, you generally give up a great deal of liquidity for this nominal tax benefit. In addition, the first years will likely have a substantial early withdrawal penalty if you need the money unexpectedly. Fairly high commissions are generally paid to those who sell these products, and the company must make up the money in some way if the client pulls out early. Administrative charges also tend to be high, after all, they usually have pretty large infrastructure to manage.

Perhaps the greatest benefit the annuities provide is lifetime income (annuity), which can be activated at after 59 1/2 years of age. The amount of the payment is based on age and the value of your account at the time. This can be a nice feature for those who would like a fixed payment in the future. There is one caveat, the company still needs to be around at that time, and while they are likely to be here if they are a reputable company, in today's changing world, anything is possible.

Universal life policies tout themselves as life insurance policies on steroids. Part of your money goes to pay for the life insurance portion of the contract, and the other portion goes to an investment vehicle of your choosing. The funds can be invested aggressively for more upside potential, or more conservatively for stability.

This product actually does make sense, except for one thing. As you get older, the portion going to insure your life (mortality cost) becomes greater, and depending on the value of investment side of contract, which is also subject to administrative charges, the entire contract could be eaten up as you get older, as mortality costs increase.

Whole life policies are supposed to be the "holy grail" of protecting your life. Not only do they cover your life if you die, but some contracts become "paid-up" after a certain time, theoretically giving you coverage for the rest of your life, without having to make additional payments. While I've no doubt several of these policies probably exist and hold true to their promises, some fall into the category of "too good to be true."

I purchased one such policy when I was 29 years old, believing it would eventually be paid up, or at the very least continue in force as long as I paid my premium. As it turns out, the illustrations provided by the company to sell the product were deceitful. The company was later sued for false misrepresentation since the policy was really a Universal Life product and not a Whole Life policy, as it was sold. The irony is that I was the licensed agent who sold myself the policy at the time on the recommendation of a golfing buddy. Oops... Live and learn!

Insurance companies are excellent in certain areas, but not so good in others. They do a great job helping us to manage risks we cannot, or are not willing, to manage ourselves, but when it comes to long-term investment vehicles, my advice is to look elsewhere.

c) Purchase Real Estate

This step, perhaps more than any other is critical to building your capital base and enabling your emotional freedom. In addition to the tremendous upside potential of real-estate as an investment over the long-term, the peace of mind you get in owning your own home is invaluable.

Once you have enough money to make a down payment, and purchase your own place to live, do it. I am not a big proponent for getting into debt in general, but now is the time to make an exception to that rule. The purchase of your home or apartment is critical for your ability to free yourself.

While there are many ways to go about buying property, and many who are willing to take your money to tell you how to do so, keep in mind these three suggestions:

1) Stretch yourself to the maximum of your ability when it comes to making your first purchase

2) Look for the least expensive place you can afford in the best part of town

3) Choose a place which will meet your needs for years to come

Decide how big of a place you need and the area of town where you want to live. Don't buy something less than your aspirations just because you have the money and can afford it. If you live in a one bedroom place now, and you are planning o have children, consider not just a two bedroom place, but at least three bedrooms. The space will come in handy and you never know, if you end up having more than one or two kids. If you do, then you can throw all the boys in one room and the girls in the other, keeping the third as your own. If you go to a two bedroom place initially, you may well have to look for something bigger before you know it. In addition, what right now may seem almost impossible for you to pay, will in time get much easier. As inflation ticks upward, and you have greater earning capacity, you will find it easier to handle your monthly mortgage payment as time goes by.

As to buying in the best part of town; it's sometimes easy to become bedazzled with the luxury of a super nice place in a terrible part of town. While there are some cases where neighborhoods turn around, and people end up making a lot of money because they get huge upside appreciation in a short period of time; do you really want to live in a dumpy part of town in the meantime? I don't think so! It may make a good investment later on, but not now.

When you are ready to purchase a home, think about your family, what it would like to get older in the area where you are considering your investment. Does it go with your personality and overall lifestyle? Can you see yourself running around with kids, taking them to activities, and going to school in the area?

Find a place where the schools, parks, and recreation areas are compatible with your way of life. Choose that area where you can see yourself maturing, and then stretch as far as you can to get there. Here you will likely be faced with a big decision in terms of how much money to borrow. Go to the limit that the bank or finance company will loan you. Do all you can to get absolutely the best place you can imaging living in for the next 15 to 20 years, and perhaps the rest of your life, if you like the area.

Does this go against what you've previously heard or thought? Likely, but think about it for a second. Do you really want to go through the hassle of moving as your family grows? Many people move often, continually "upgrading", and taking out higher and higher loans, to pay more interest, and get bigger tax breaks. This is idiotic in my way of seeing things; but more on this later.

My primary intention is for you to become debt-free, financially sound and independent. Purchasing a property, which also serves as your principle residence, is a big part of this overall strategy. As time goes by and you earn more money, you can accelerate payments, paying off the entire note, and owning the property free and clear in record time. If you do so, you have the added advantage of being able to use your property as collateral for a loan if you have an emergency, since the banks and finance companies will line up to give you credit when you own your own home free and clear.

Purchasing your home will likely be a cornerstone to your overall plan enabling you to free yourself. Real estate provides many outstanding additional options to invest your money, many of which can fund themselves, eventually paying of the loans and then providing you with a steady stream of income. The options are endless and well worth exploring. If I were a young man going into business, I would seriously consider real estate as a career, not just for the commissions to be made from selling property, but to become my own best client for additional purchases.

Another benefit of owing your own home outright is that you get the emotional advantage of knowing no one can ever come and kick you out. As long as you pay our taxes and don't do anything completely stupid, you will be okay. As a bare minimum you will have a place to lay down at night and a roof over your head.

d) Get Debt Free

Being debt free sets you well on your way to be free financially and emotionally. In a world where we wear our credit scores on our breast like a badge of honor, getting in debt and staying there, has become a way of life for many people in developed countries.

I'm not against getting into debt to acquire the things we really need and cannot get with our own capital, but once you pay off the debt, keep it that way.

We are often advised to "trade-up" to a larger home, paying more interest charges so we can get a larger tax break for the additional interest we pay. Let's cut this myth to the quick, right here with this example:

1. "Trade up" to a bigger place costing more money

2. Pay $10,000 more in interest (larger loan)

3. In 30% tax bracket you save you $3,000

4. Net cost to you $7,000

Getting into a larger home, with a more expensive loan will cost you more money, regardless of the tax breaks. Granted, you can live in a bigger and better place, but this also equates to more responsibility. This is why I suggest buying a residence where you will be able to live for years to come.

Once you no longer owe any money to anyone, for

any reason, you begin to breathe a little easier, and walk a little taller. Being debt-free is as much of a psychological load off our mind as a financial weight lifted off our pocket book. When you own everything free and clear, have a way to make money today, and have a capital base beneath you, you are positioned to free yourself. There is only one step to go.

3) Insure Yourself

Much of what I say in this section is likely to go against what you believe to be true about insurance. The truth of the matter is that everyone is different, and while I am confident you can insure yourself against many of the risks you will face in your lifetime, you may not be willing to do so. If you are the kind of person who likes to file a claim whenever any little thing goes wrong, or takes a certain joy in getting the "better" of the insurance company by getting more money back from them than you give them, then you might as well stop reading this section right now. Take my advice on inspiring yourself and investing in yourself, become debt-free, and call it a day.

If, on the other hand, you are tired of fueling the coffers of a multi-billion dollar industry with your hard-earned money, then stick around. I am not against insurance companies, on the contrary, I believe they provide a very valuable and needed service to cover the risks we cannot, or are not willing to cover ourselves.

Starting out on our path in life, insurance is likely to be an important part of our overall financial plan. Later on in life, as your priorities and necessities change, and also as you build your capital base, the amount of risk you are willing to bear can also change. This is why it's vital we constantly review our situation, evaluating which risks we can cover and which we delegate to an insurance company.

Before we get into the nuts and bolts of specific types of insurance policies, let's talk about the insurance companies themselves. Like any other corporation, as we've already discussed, their chief goal is to make a profit. The truth of the matter is that we are all better off when they are profitable, because when they are not, ultimately we are the ones who will suffer when it's time to make a claim if they are unable to pay. Notwithstanding, I prefer the insurance company not make too much money off of me, particularly if it is on a risk I can manage myself without their intervention.

It is important to emphasize that not buying insurance DOES NOT mean you are "self-insured," on the contrary, it simply means you are "uninsured." There is a very big difference between the two. To insure yourself, you plan for the worst case scenario, and then do what you can to create the best.

Remember, insurance companies pay claims when something bad happens. Part of the insurance game requires that we prove to the insurance company we are entitled to a claim based on the coverage we purchased. If not, we are SOL (simply out of luck). Here is where it is very important to read the small print before signing any contract, especially insurance policies.

I know what you are probably thinking... "No one reads those things!" This is precisely the reason why you should read the small print. When you realize the number of exceptions and stipulations most insurance policies have, you might think twice about paying the premiums you hate to pay, but pay anyway because you feel you must.

Instead, you can choose to insure yourself for those risks you can handle both financially and emotionally, delegating those you cannot to an insurance company. It's not always wise to insure yourself, and depending on your situation, it can be financial suicide.

With each of the different types of insurance we will discuss, we will examine two factors regarding whether or not you can "handle" a specific risk. The first is the financial, or monetary side of the equation; the other is the emotional side. The economic side is quite simple. Two plus two equals four. Either the capital base you have built allows you to cover a particular risk, or it won't. You are in or out, with no shades of gray.

The emotional side of the equation is quite different, and not as easy to quantify. Here two plus two doesn't always equal four. Sometimes it is less, while others it is more. It may make perfect financial sense to insure yourself for a particular risk, but your emotional side may rebel, not accepting the risk, despite reason.

It's interesting to note that you can buy insurance to cover just about any risk you can possibly imagine. If there is risk involved, there will likely be some company or individual willing to cover that risk for you. From body parts and organs to art and gun collections, just about anything can be insured. Obviously, the premium charged to cover the event is commensurate with the risk. The company will always make sure to not only cover their costs, but also leave a room for a profit.

Some people believe they should be insured for

just about everything under the sun that can possibly go wrong. If you are one of those people, then go ahead and buy the insurance. There are many companies vying for your hard-earned cash. With this said, there is a better way for you, your family, and your loved ones to benefit more from your efforts, rather than continuing to fuel an enormous industry which depends on fear as the primary motivating force behind their existence.

Let's look at this logically for a moment, from a business perspective. The actuaries (very smart people who run around insurance companies figuring out the likelihood of certain events) know with a high degree of probability how much a particular risk will cost the company. If they have a group of 100 people, they have a pretty good idea how many of them will get sick, make a car claim, or have their house burn down. Once they figure out how much money they need from the group to cover the risk, they simply add to that number several items, including: administrative costs, commissions, rent, electricity, phones, investment in technology, taxes, and of course as much as possible for stockholders. The end result is the premium we must pay the insurance company to cover a specific risk.

Insurance companies are experts in analyzing and covering these risks that otherwise many of us would be unable to cover ourselves. But there is a fundamental reason behind our continual need for insurance companies to protect us. By in large we are too undisciplined to build a capital base to cover losses ourselves. Unless you have the wherewithal do so, you will be hopelessly tied to the insurance companies and they will continue to feed on the fear they peddle.

For those risks you decide to delegate, there are many fine reputable insurance companies around. Do your homework and find the one that works best for your needs and the risk you need to cover; but plan on slowly beginning to eliminate these payments as you become more successful in building your capital base.

Once you get to the point when you are saving not only the normal 10% you are accustomed to saving, but also the amount you would typically pay when you self insure, your emergency fund grows even quicker, giving you more of a cushion to insure yourself for more things.

Another way you can save on your insurance premiums is by raising the deductibles and/or extending waiting periods before coverage initiates, when your capital base allows you to do so.

Perhaps one the biggest obstacles to freeing yourself from financial slavery to others is to be willing to put your diapers aside, put on your big boy or girl underwear, and take responsibility for your decisions. I'm convinced that many financial institutions and insurance companies exist for the simple reason that we love to blame someone else if something goes wrong.

By forcing ourselves to take responsibility for our failures, and credit for our successes, we take away an escape valve we are accustomed to having. When we insure ourselves, we begin to take better care of what we own and how we choose to spend our money.

Insurance has a purpose and you should use it as

a part of your overall financial plan, but it need not play a dominant role. In short, as we build our capital base, we become better equipped to handle losses we would otherwise need to insure.

For most types of insurance, we have three options:

1) We can decide not to pay the insurance, praying for the best and doing nothing for the worst

2) We can pay the insurance, planning for the worst and hoping for the best

3) We can insure ourselves, expecting the best and preparing the worse

The first option is just silly. Are you in or out? Make a decision, don't get caught with your pants down, it could be one of the worst decisions of your life. The second option should be used for any risk we cannot handle financially or unwilling to handle emotionally, simply pay to cover the risk and hope for the best. The third option is our holy grail. Let's plan for and expect the best things in life, but be prepared for the worst.

a) Determine Your Level of Risk

When we look at insurance, as is the case with investing in ourselves, we need to determine our own risk tolerance, and there is no "right" level of risk. In fact, it's a very personal thing and likely to be different for everyone.

While insuring yourself may seem like a big gamble, the truth is whenever the insurance company insures us for something, they are betting on something GOOD happening to us, and we are betting on something BAD happening.

Have you ever thought about this? If you are an insurance company, you love people who never have anything go wrong. The only time we need insurance, or use it, is when something bad happens. Insurance claims are made when things don't work, are stolen, get burnt, we have an accident, we get sick, or we die.

When we give an insurance company our money, we are effectively betting something will go wrong, and hoping for the best. When we insure ourselves, we are betting on the best of outcomes, while preparing for the worst.

The irony is that the insurance companies hope, and fully expect, we will be okay most of the time. As long as not too much happens to us, or too often, they are happy to take our money to cover the risk. Besides, as I have already mentioned, they are very good at determining how much they need to charge not only to pay for any claims, but also to pay all their expenses and leave a profit for their shareholders.

Can you imagine a world without insurance? For all of us, there was a time when we we were unaware of the concept. As a child, if another kid stole your toy, you either grabbed it back, or you were out of luck. You had little recourse. If you were shy, you likely said or did nothing, letting them have it; while if you were more aggressive, you probably took it back.

In most schools there are bullies who take what the want from the meek. The case in point is similar. The insurance companies are the "bullies" who take what they want, and we are the "meek" who do as we are told. The difference is how they portray themselves. The insurance company presents itself as the savior to all the bad things that can happen to us, while constantly feeding our consciousness with the fear of what might someday happen. They know that as long as they keep sowing fear into our minds, they will keep reaping the benefit of the money we give them.

Most interesting is that they want you to be healthy, wealthy, and wise. As long as you are in good shape, you make no claims, and they continue to make money, taking it from you like candy from a baby. You may kick and scream a bit, but in the end you pay.

If you were positive nothing bad would ever happen to you, there would be no reason to buy insurance. The fact of the matter is that we are not always as healthy, wealthy, or as wise as we would like to be. Like it or not, bad things will happen to us. We will get robbed, our health will fail, emergencies will make us spend our hard-earned money, and there will be times when our faith will be tested beyond belief. I'm not trying to be negative, just realistic about expectations. It is for these times most of us pay insurance companies to protect us.

In exchange for covering a particular risk, we give the insurance company our money, in the form of a premium. It's a fair exchange, except for the fact that they have the deck stacked heavily in their favor. In Las Vegas, the margins favoring the house are generally slim. In many cases their advantage is a mere 51% for them against 49% for us. Insurance companies work on larger margins, and perhaps well they should! I don't know about you, but if I choose an insurance to cover me for a particular risk, I want to make sure they are around if, and when, I need them. I just don't want them making so much money off of me in the meantime.

Not buying insurance in many of the instances we are about to talk about is financial suicide at best, doomed to failure from the beginning. We should have insurance to cover certain things, but let's be smart about it. This is where our risk tolerance level becomes so important.

Some people in Las Vegas go straight to the slot machines, comfortable with a fairly simple and straightforward way to try their luck. They see lights and sounds all around, along with a few people winning every once in a while, and they are happy with the One Armed Bandits to see if they can come away a winner.

Many head for the Black Jack tables, Roulette, Craps or perhaps take a spin on the Wheel of Fortune. The more adventurous go for Poker and Baccarat, where they test their skill against other players, though of course, the house always gets a cut. Others sit around in bars and betting pits, wagering on he outcomes of just about any game or event taking place in the world.

What is the common ingredient?

They all have an element of risk. Some of the games seem to have better odds for us than others. Some create emotion and energy we like to be around, others mesmerize us with the hoopla of people. Between one thing and another, we can end up dropping a lot of cash in a very short period of time on any of these games.

Then, there are those who go to Las Vegas to watch others gamble, enjoying the other things this fabulous city has to offer. If you are one of these, then stick with me, because this about my speed in Las Vegas. I'm definitely not a gambler at heart.

As is the case with most people, I don't like to lose money. Well, I've got news for you, neither do the insurance companies; so it only makes sense to act more like they do when choosing to insure ourselves, basing our decision on the numbers, and paying less attention to their scare tactics. Make no doubt about it, choosing to insure ourselves is a should be a business decision, but necessarily as human beings there is an emotional element as well.

As soon as we make our first major purchase, we are generally faced with the question of whether or not to buy insurance. In many cases, we have just made a huge effort to purchase something which was not easy for us to buy. Sometimes all the salesman needs to ask is, "I assume you will want to insure your purchase against loss?"

As we stand their with our credit card in hand, and people waiting behind us, we ask the details of the insurance. After hemming and hawing for a moment, weighing the cost of the coverage with the value of the item, we either purchase the insurance or we do not. It's not an exact science, sometimes it may sound good and we buy it, other times we decide to pass.

Two things are happening here. The first is that they are planting the seed of fear in your mind that something might go wrong with your purchase. The second is that even if you don't buy the insurance, you walk away wondering if you should have done so.

What I can assure you is of one thing. The insurance company has thought very long and hard about the coverage they are offering to you, and the risk to them if you make a claim. When they quote a premium, they have covered the risk of loss, together with commissions, administrative costs, and all kinds of other things you never even imagined existed. Well, maybe I'm exaggerating a little, but not much. There are a lot of people running around in insurance companies, doing all kinds of different jobs. Someone has to pay them, do you want it to be you?

So here's the thing, take their advice and use it when making a decision on whether or not to insure yourself. After analyzing the situation carefully, determine if you can handle the risk financially and emotionally. If so, then insure yourself, if not then transfer the risk to the insurance company. Easy peasy...

Try this idea on for size first with small things. Look at extended warranties, renters insurance, property insurance, and liability insurance (when not required by law). Life, disability, and health insurance are more difficult to cover, but not impossible. We will cover each of these items in the following sections.

The insurance company tells you the approximate risk by the amount of money they charge in the form of the premium we have to pay. Many think erroneously that they can insure themselves by simply putting aside the money you would normally pay to the insurance company. This may work some of the time, but certainly not all the time. It will likely not be enough to cover many of the losses we might face. This is why we should add to the normal amount we invest in ourselves, the amount of the premiums for insurance we are offered, but refuse. Critical here is the capital base we have built as an emergency fund to cover losses we would normally look to the insurance company to cover.

There is a reason why only paying ourselves the premium we would normally pay to the insurance company will not always work. They are spreading the risk over a much greater population. For example: They may well know that 4 or 5 people in a group of 100 will make a claim for a particular event, but here's the catch. They don't know which of the hundred will be affected. If we insure ourselves and happen to be one of the four or five, we can get burned in a heartbeat, if we don't have the capital to cover the loss.

The key to being able to insure yourself is having a sufficient capital base, and then add on to it by coverages you choose to manage yourself. If you have no base now you may find it hard to imagine having money, but if you save 10% of everything you earn, and put it away without thinking about it or using it, you will soon have money, it's simple math. If you dip into it because of any one of a million temptations out there catches your fancy, you will not. This isn't rocket science we're talking about here.

I've said it before, and I will say it again. Not buying insurance is not the same as being self insured. Self insured means you have the wherewithal to cover the event financially and emotionally. This is where our risk tolerance comes in, since both factors must come together in our decision. We may have the ability to cover a risk financially, but not emotionally, or vice versa.

Could you start all over, if you didn't buy flood insurance and your house was wiped away in a flood? Some people can handle that risk, others can't. Financially speaking it is merely a matter of numbers, but the emotional ramifications are tremendous.

Could you, and would you be willing to start all over again if your home was wiped out and you didn't have insurance?

Would you be able to handle the storm season each year which batters your property without mercy knowing you would have to pay for the repairs?

Some people might say, "No problem, if it gets knocked down, I have the ability to build another one. Besides, it might be fun to have a new place." Others might say, "I can't stand the thought of having to start all over again without financial assistance."

Measuring this risk isn't a mathematical equation. Each decision we take has a risk. If the emotional risk of a loss would break you spiritually, despite having funds to cover it, buy the insurance! Don't think twice about it. In fact, I have a very good insurance agent who can help you out, and he's a very nice guy.

We need insurance for much of what we do, but not for everything. If you can't bear the thought of going to the doctor and not getting the office visit reimbursed through insurance, you might want to stop reading this section and jump to the end right now, if you haven't already; but if you are tired of diverting your funds into the coffers of a multi-billion dollar industry that is betting on you being pretty much okay in the years to come, then stop doing it, you have a choice.

My insurance agent loves to use one of industry's very favorite sayings:

"It's better to have insurance and not need it, than to need it and not have it."

I'd say, well yes... this is true sometimes, but not always. If I am planning on being "okay" most of the time, why would I bet on something bad happening to me by paying an insurance company? Besides, they even do the math for me to give an indication of about how much we need to pay to cover the risk. They make it easy by giving us the numbers.

If you see a premium which is particularly high for a event you want to cover, then you can bet they believe their is a lot of risk involved; that's why they are charging so much. Try getting Sky Diving insurance. You probably can get it, but it might cost you an arm and a leg.

Here's an idea... How about if:

- You do everything in our power not to get mugged, by being more aware of your surroundings and taking self-defense classes?

- You take your home's security seriously, by protecting the perimeter with "Smith & Wesson," along with instruction on how to use the new security system?

- You protect your family by insuring your life as long as we are the primary bread winner for your family?

- You save money and develop a way to make money, in case you you are out of work or have a disability?

- You pay for health insurance, as needed and when required by law, but raise deductibles and waiting periods to decrease costs?

- Life is a risk. Every time we go out the door in the morning, there's a chance we may not come back as planned in the evening.

Sh.....

It happens...

The car doesn't work, the train is late, the buses go on strike, and the kids get sick; often at the same time. Determine your risk tolerance, then cover the risks you can afford financially and emotionally by insuring yourself; transferring the risk of the rest to a good insurance company, plain and simple.

i) Extended Warranties

Let's start with the risks which are easier to cover

and work our way to those more difficult to handle. A big money maker for insurance companies throughout the world is the extended warranties they provide for everything from toaster ovens to new vehicles.

We need to understand how the insurance company works and how they do business. They make decisions based on cold, hard facts, with little or no emotions in the process. On the other hand, they sell their products based on the fear. They remind us how terrible it feels to buy something and then later find out it doesn't meet our expectations or have it stolen from us.

If the product is defective, we usually find out fairly quickly and in many cases the product is covered by the manufacturer against initial defects. This is an important starting point. If a product doesn't offer some kind of money back guarantee, or replacement guarantee, it's a good idea to test it before buying it.

If we are confident we want to go through with the purchase, right about the time the cashier is taking our debit or credit card to pay for the purchase, they ask, "You do want to buy the extended warranty—" here they typically lower their voice an octave, and add, "don't you?"

In many cases the change of inflection in their voice and the fear they instill are enough for us to give our assent to buy the insurance without further ado. In other cases, we will ask what the insurance covers and the general conditions. Here we are often met with a well-rehearsed speech, indicating all the reasons why we should buy the extra coverage, and how foolish we would be to refuse it.

Am I exaggerating?

I don't think so. Employees are often compensated on their ability to successfully sell this type of insurance, and the more adept they are, the more they benefit from the additional income dangled in front of their faces. It's easy money to be had, I would do the same, wouldn't you?

Let's look at their primary tactic, fear.

Plain and simple, they do their best to scare the heck out of us into taking the extra coverage they are offering. If we refuse, they may lower their head, look at us over the top of their glasses, and shake their heads. "It'd be a shame if this nice, shiny new ##### (enter the name of whatever we are buying) were to get stolen, damaged, or broken."

All of the sudden, we have flashbacks of everything we have ever had stolen, as well as everything we have ever had damaged or broken. As the salesperson sees us rocking back in forth between purchasing the insurance or not, they slip in the following comment:

"If you figure it out over the life of the guarantee, it only costs a few pennies per day."

In many cases, this is all the additional encouraging we need, after all, what are a few pennies a day for peace of mind? Despite our initial intention of not buying the insurance, we suddenly find ourselves nodding in agreement, like the little dogs we used to put in the back of car windows back in the day.

While this type coverage can range from a few dollars to thousands of dollars, the insurance company is betting that you never will have to make a claim, and if you do, that it will be within the risk parameters they have already established for the coverage. Most of the time they are right. This is the reason they continue to make money hand over fist, buying some of the best real estate and building some of the tallest buildings all over the world. They know with a pretty high rate of certainty how many people will make a claim on a particular policy and how much it will cost them.

While the risk of losing your precious new purchase is scary, think carefully about what you are doing when you purchase an extended warranty. You are betting something bad will happen to the item you are purchasing, and the insurance company is betting everything will be okay.

When it comes to extending that warranty, it's important to be aware of several things. The first is that if we do have a claim, we must be able to prove the loss is covered according to the terms and conditions of the insurance policy and comply with their procedure to make a claim. If we have something stolen, we will most likely need to file a police report. Original receipts and proof of coverage are usually part of their protocol as well. In many instances, people will forget they even bought insurance for an item, and if they do remember they have coverage, may very well give up early in the process of making a claim, unless they have everything they need at hand, or if it is for a high dollar amount.

As soon as the insurance company gets the claim, they will review it and determine whether or not it is valid. They have every right to refuse coverage for items not specifically mentioned in the contract and they will likely make you comply to the letter in terms of the claim procedure. They would be silly not to do this since it helps them to avoid frivolous or fraudulent claims.

Consider how we care for items that are insured as opposed to those that are not. A cell phone with insurance to replace it if it is lost or stolen, is prone to get beat up pretty badly; while one without insurance often will travel only in a special case designed to protect it, and be carefully taken care of by its owner.

How about taking better care of the things you buy, and foregoing the extended warranty programs, unless the risk you are covering is more than you can handle financially or emotionally? As you will see, in each of our examples, this is the final litmus test to see whether or not we can insure ourselves, or if we choose to transfer the risk to an insurance company.

If we can afford the risk financially, but emotionally can't bear the thought of having to disburse money for the same product again, then consider purchasing the insurance. Not everyone has the mentality to be able to insure themselves, but it is almost always an option, particularly when it has to do with extended warranties.

If you are careful with the things you own and you

stick to your investment plan, over time if you are likely come out ahead, but rest assured there will be challenges as you go forward. As long as you are prepared for them financially and emotionally, you can begin to to insure yourself for certain risks, decreasing your dependence on insurance companies.

ii) Car Insurance

To drive a motor vehicle in most places requires you to have at least liability insurance for third parties. This is a given, if you are going to drive, you must have it, no questions asked.

Full coverage on your vehicle covering its loss or damage will likely be required if you have an outstanding loan. Once you finish paying the loan, you can decide whether or not to keep full coverage, opting only to take only liability coverage, as required by law.

When can we self insure our own automobiles?

We go back to our rule of thumb. If you can afford to completely lose the vehicle, or make a major repair, and also deal with the incident emotionally, then insure it yourself. If not, delegate the risk to an insurance company, they will be happy take your money from you and assume the risk.

Let's take a look for a moment at the psychology of car insurance. For the sake of argument, let's suppose that we have a vehicle worth $20,000, and the premium to insure the vehicle will cost us 10% or $2,000, per year. Under normal circumstances the company knows that the $2,000 per year you and others in the group pay, will be enough to pay for claims in that year by the group. Perhaps you have no claims for three years, so you have given the company $6,000. From your point of view, if the cost of the repair is less than the $6,000, we would have been better off insuring ourselves, if it over this amount, then paying the insurance will have been to our advantage since we are getting back more than we paid in.

The insurance company, however, doesn't see it this way. They take in premiums to manage certain types of risk for a particular group of people, for a certain period of time. In this case the risk is something bad could happen to your vehicle. They know that claims on a red Ferrari driven by a young male are likely to be much higher than those made on a blue Honda Civic driven by a little old lady to church on Sundays. They will price the risk accordingly. The young man will likely have to pay an arm and a leg for insurance, whereas the little old lady may only have to give an eye, or a finger (nudge, nudge, wink, wink... are you paying attention?).

The insurance company covers a specific event, in this case damage to the vehicle, for a specific time period, usually one year. When the company takes your money, they put it into a reserve fund along with all of the funds received with a similar risk. Until the end of the year, the premiums charged are available to pay any claims by anyone in the group. Only after the time period is over does the company integrate those premiums into their books as earned capital.

They really aren't too concerned if we have been a client for a short or long period of time, though they would like us to think it makes a difference. Don't believe me? Try going ten or twenty years with the same insurance company for your automobile with no claims, and then have two or three consecutive claims in one year to see how they adjust your next year's premium. They view the business on a year by year and a case by case basis, analyzing the risk anew with each renewal to make sure it is still profitable to the company, if it's not, they will simply stop offering the coverage.

If you have many claims over a short period of time, the company is likely to either raise the premium substantially or refuse coverage all together. When you insure yourself, you don't have to treat yourself this way! You can be a "kinder and gentler" type of insurer. More on this later.

If your vehicle is five years old and depreciating in value quickly but still running fine, consider not making the expenditure for a new vehicle. Think of all the repairs you can make with the monthly costs of you new vehicle you save. You also avoid a new loan, increased insurance premiums, and a whole new round of the costs associated with purchasing a new car. Instead, you can choose to take care of the car you have which is now paid for, insure it yourself, and pay the obligatory liability insurance in case you do something stupid. This is, of course, assuming you have already built up your emergency fund which you can use to replace the vehicle if it is stolen or fix it if it is damaged.

This brings us to the emotional part of the equation. Are you prepared mentally to deal with a complete loss or major repair if something goes wrong? Despite having a capital base, some people can't imagine sustaining that type of a risk from an emotional standpoint.

As a final note on insuring your own vehicles, and as I just mentioned in the previous section, we tend to treat the items differently depending on whether they fully covered with paid insurance or if we self insure them. Notice how someone treats their vehicle if they have full insurance coverage and a low deductible, and then observe someone whose car is self insured. The first will not think twice about driving aggressively or parking the car anywhere, since they are generally not too concerned with nicks and scratches, since they can get them fixed for "free" by the insurance company. Those who are self insured tend to drive more defensively and to take much better care of where they park their vehicle, since they do their best to keep "stripes on the tiger" to a bare minimum. While it should be obvious, if you are going to assume the risk of insuring your own vehicle, make sure you do your best to take care of it.

We often take it for granted that we must insure everything we own. If the asset is worth a lot of money in comparison to our overall capital base, then by all means transfer the risk to a reputable insurance company, but if you can handle the loss of, or damage to the asset financially and emotionally, then insure it yourself.

I mentioned this example to my insurance agent and he told me something very interesting. He said it is quite common for people who are very wealthy and who have many vehicles to self insure them. They know that if they lose vehicle through theft or an accident, they can replace it by buying another without too much financial hardship.

Measure the risk associated with your vehicles in terms of their value and your capital base to determine whether or not you can assume the risk. If you can, then insure them yourself.

iii) Homeowner's / Renter's Insurance

We often assume it is absolutely necessary to have home owner's or rental insurance. In the case of the homeowners insurance, we are likely to be required to have it if we have a mortgage; whereas in the case of renter's insurance, it is up to us whether or not we buy the coverage.

Many people who have been paying home owner's insurance since they first purchased their homes cannot possibly imagine going without it. Others have been induced to purchase rental insurance to protect their valuables. I'm not saying you shouldn't have these coverages, just don't assume you absolutely have to have them.

Remember the primary sales tactic for insurance companies is fear. If they can scare us into believing many bad things can happen to us, we will pay them thousands of dollars over our lifetime to insure ourselves in case they do. So they keep scaring us and we keep paying.

Instead of making decisions based on fear and emotion, we can instead base our decision on cold, hard facts, as the insurance company does. Make the decision based on dollars, cents, and some common sense.

By looking at the amount an insurance company charges to cover a particular risk, we can find out how likely they believe the event is to occur. If you are being charged a high amount to insure against your home against floods in comparison to other areas, there is probably a good reason for it. You may be on a flood plain. Be wary of taking this type of risk unless you are sure you can handle the risk financially and emotionally.

Some people can handle certain losses from a financial standpoint, but break down on the emotional front. Most of us would be devastated if we lose their home to a flood, earthquake, tornado, or some alien laser. The majority of us would likely be unable to bounce back from a tragedy of that magnitude without insurance. Then there are others who might simply shake their heads in disbelief, dust themselves off, look for someone to help them, and get started building their home again as soon as possible, taking it step buy step.

Until you have sufficient capital, you are not likely to be able replace your entire home, so it may take awhile for you to assume this risk, but if you have the confidence in your ability to make money, you may be closer than you think. More important than having money in the bank is our ability to make it if we need it. If you have the ability to make money, you can lose everything today, and begin start again tomorrow.

As your capital grows, you will be able to handle many the smaller repairs you previously expected your insurance company to cover. Broken windows, leaky pipes, electrical problems, and many other things can be handled by your emergency fund of 3 to 6 months. As your financial capacity to handle difficulty grows, you can analyze the risk of your particular situation and insure yourself when you are able to do so.

iv) Disability / Life Insurance

While disability and life insurance cover different risks, we can talk about them together. Most of us don't like to think about death or disability, yet they are a reality of life. Turning a blind eye to them could create hardship for your family if you are the primary bread winner and something should happen to you. Since these risks can be a difficult to cover ourselves, often the best way to cover them is through an insurance company.

Statistically speaking, you are more likely to become disabled and unable to work, than to die; so disability insurance can be an important part of your overall strategy if you have others who depend on your income. If you are working and have an employer, they often pay for this insurance, if not you can contract it separately. One of the determinants regarding the premium you pay is the waiting period before the insurance starts paying. The longer the waiting period, usually the lower the premium. As you build up your emergency fund to 3 to 6 months of your income, you can extend this period to save money.

By the way, being "disabled" does not mean you are not "able" to make money anymore. In fact, many people who are disabled make a lot of money despite their limitations. This poses an interesting question you should ask yourself. If you were to become disabled, and unable to work at your present job, what could you do to make money?

Though making money seems to mystify many of us, it really isn't all that difficult. All we need to do is buy something for a dollar, sell it for two, and then do it again, and again, and again. While it is nice to think we will get a disability check if we are disabled, better is to have an option where you can make your own money should you need it. Once you have a way to make money, even if you become incapacitated physically, then you have just created your own disability insurance. If it involves "living what you love," then congratulations, you are in the bonus round!

If you have a young family and have debt, then purchase life insurance. The amount you choose to purchase is also a very personal choice. Some people suggesting buying an amount equal to 20 times your current income. If you do this, your family can live in the lap of luxury, living off the interest of your inheritance. My suggestion would be to make sure your children are ready for life and pay off your principal residence. This way they will have a roof over their head and the ability to deal with life's difficulties on their own.

So now we come to the question of what type of life insurance policy to buy. Here you can get all kinds of opinions. If the advice comes from your insurance agent, the answer will most likely be Whole Life Insurance or Universal Life Insurance, the second of which combines life insurance coverage with an investment. These two products pay among the highest commissions to producers, and as often tends to be the case, they follow the money.

Since I became an investment advisor, in 1985, investment professionals have been suggesting the best strategy for life insurance is to buy Term Life Insurance and then invest the difference. In my opinion, this still seems to be the best advice. When you are younger term insurance tends to be fairly inexpensive, and you can cover the specific risk you want for a specified period of time and then be done with it. You can handle the investment side of the equation as I suggest in the section on invest in yourself, or you can choose a trusted investment advisor to lead you through the process.

The battle over which type of life insurance is best to buy will likely continue long after you and I are both gone. Each side will defend their option as the best, and quite frankly any option you choose is better than none at all. Saving money is important but even your insurance agent has to make a living somehow. Perhaps the best part of having life insurance is the peach of mind it gives you as you go out into the world daily to do whatever it is you do.

Once your children are educated, have a way to make a living, and you are debt-free; then you can often assume the risk for both disability and life insurance yourself. It may be difficult for you to imagine right now how you could do this, particularly if you are one of those people who has more "month than income," or who have their entire income spent before it ever arrives; but if you follow my advice by investing in yourself first, you will begin to slowly build a capital base. In time, you will be able to save money by assuming many of the risks you now transfer to an insurance company.

As to whether or not to self insure these two risks yourself, we go back to our rule of thumb:

If you can assume the risk financially of not being able to work, and can take care of your family if you die, then you are well on your way. Being prepared for disability and/or death are difficult subjects and not to be taken lightly. If you couldn't get up tomorrow and do what you have always done to make money and survive, what would you do? How will you deal with the ultimate fate we all face. How will you deal with your demise?

Think about what you would do if everything went to hell in a hand basket. Prepare for the worst by building a capital base and a way to provide income if you become disabled, then expect good things to happen. Don't worry about whether you might become disabled, but be ready if it does. Don't be concerned about how your family will get by if you are not around, but plan to have things taken care of if necessary. Set yourself free by expecting the best and being prepared for the worst.

v) Medical Insurance

Okay, here we go, this is the big one. Health care and the costs associated with it are a huge issue for most nations around the world. In the United States, the government has gone so far as to make it obligatory for everyone to have health insurance. While concept is interesting, I don't think it will hold. Making something that has to do with our own bodies obligatory in a free country just somehow seems wrong to me. I understand what they are trying to do, but it doesn't seem to be working, as health care costs continue to skyrocket, and I wonder if care is any better.

Why should we be told what to do with our bodies if, and when, we get sick? Must we always follow their system?

Seems to me the whole system is rigged to find something wrong with us. Kind of like going into the mechanic and asking if anything is wrong with the car. They will find something wrong. The same seems to be happening in health care. A variety of tests are generally run to determine what they need to fix, take out, or replace. Once they do figure it out, they don't let go, and we are lucky if we ever get out of the system. After all, as long as we keep going in for more medical visits, they keep making money.

Would it be so much as to just let people die with dignity at home when their time comes? Must we always poke and prod them to see what's wrong?

Why must death be something we want to prolong at all costs? What about if we lived our life in a way that if we were to die tomorrow, we could do so with no regrets?

This is a difficult subject to talk for many of us and we all have our own opinions. As for me, if I get really sick, I'm wondering if its not better to just stay home, grin and bear it, be surrounded by those I love, and perhaps a dog or two, until I'm done.

Medical insurance often forces people into a multi-billion dollar industry which is driven by profit. I'm sure most of the companies are also interested in providing effective health care, but fact of the matter is that they must turn out a profit. If they don't, plain and simple, they won't be around very long.

Let's look at medical insurance from a strict business standpoint. What if instead of paying the insurance company, instead we were to instead use the same amount of money to prevent getting sick, with a healthy diet, lots of exercise, and periodic checks to a trusted medical professional of our choosing? This seems like a better alternative.

Yet it won't work in many cases because people simply won't invest the money in themselves to be healthier from the get go. They will still get sick, have to go to the hospital, and we are right back where we started.

Health care is a difficult issue and I don't claim to have all the answers. My aim is to simply make some sense of the mess. Before we dig in, let me say that the risk of insuring yourself for medical coverage is HUGE, so tread CAREFULLY before handling this risk yourself.

For all my tirades against the big evil insurance companies, and their obvious underlying desire to rule the world, they do provide a VERY NEEDED service. It is difficult for us to insure ourselves with the same effectiveness they do for one simple reason. The insurance company spreads their risk over many individuals, so they are relatively sure they will not get burned. Before you have built a sufficient capital base, if you have a major medical event, the fickle finger of fate can easily choose you, and if it does, it could destroy you financially. Never fool yourself into believing something might not happen to you. We can look at anyone, in any station in life, anywhere in the world, and say: "But for the grace of God, there go I." What happens to other people could very well happen to us, so we should be prepared for the worst.

While we may be required to have medical coverage (as is the case currently in the USA), our cost will depend on many different factors. Among the most important are the deductibles we pay and the coverages we choose. Generally speaking, the lower the deductible and the more extensive the coverage, the higher will be the cost.

As our capital base increases, allowing us to handle small expenses, we can raise our deductibles and be more selective with the coverages we choose. I don't know about you, but when I think about a policy covering millions and millions of dollars, I wonder how many times they are going to have to poke and prod my body to generate that kind of revenue!

In any event, with this as a base, let's look at insuring ourselves in the context of medical insurance. As is the case with all the insurances we have talked about so far, doing nothing is always an option, but in this of all cases, doing nothing could literally wipe you out, so be very careful! Do not consider going without insurance because you don't have the money. If you don't have enough money to pay for coverage, you probably need it more than ever.

Determine the your needs and those of your family. Carefully determine how much you can afford financially if one of your tribe gets sick. How will you deal with the situation emotionally? Choose your deductibles and coverage accordingly, but definitely DO NOT simply go without health insurance because you can't afford it. I understand that one of the primary causes of bankruptcy in the USA is the inability to pay health-care bills.

With many medical interventions costing thousands, and in some cases millions of dollars, insuring yourself for medical problems is not for the faint of heart, and if you are already suffering from major medical issues and are currently insured, take care with the words you are about to read.

On the other hand, if you are just a normal person who is fairly healthy and does his or her best to eat well, exercise, and live a healthy life, my words may be of great benefit to reduce your costs while at the same time opening your mind to different health care alternatives.

Insurance agents are always quick to point out the claims they have had recently from their clients and how much the insurance company paid out in each instance. This is one of their tools of the trade. The examples they use validate their product and create fear of having to face a similar situation without insurance. They remind us that we are mortal and that accidents can happen. For most of us, a few of these stories, and we are ready to pay the premium for another year. I'm convinced insurance agents are there to remind us the risk is real, and don't kid yourself, it is very real.

Yet most often nothing happens, but we continue to bet on something bad happening, by buying insurance. If we were positive we would never need any kind of medical attention, it would be silly for us to pay for medical insurance, unless of course, we are obligated by the government to do so. Yet, the truth of the matter is that we will get sick, and practically all of us know someone who has had some kind of a serious medical procedure, costing more money than we can ever possibly imagine spending.

Being this the case, we should have some kind of health insurance coverage. If we cannot cover the risk ourselves, it's important to transfer the risk to the insurance company and choose the right coverage for our situation. Let's take a little closer look at two typical types of medical insurance coverage you might find:

1. Full coverage for 2 million dollars per year with a low deductible and a high premium

2. Limited coverage for extreme cases capped at $1,000,000 per year with a high deductible and a low premium

The first option appears to be better, but let's take a closer look. In the first case, we get wonderful coverage for all kinds of illnesses, but it comes at a price. Depending on where you live in the world, the cost ranges from hundreds to thousands of dollars per year.

On a policy like the first option, I was recently quoted $6,000 per year, or about $500 per month for an international policy covering myself and my wife. Your cost is likely to be much different depending on your age, health, and country of residence, but it serves as a basis of comparison.

The second option costs $1,200 per year, or about $100 per month. If you have a capital base, the second option can save you quite a bit of money up front, but it can also cost you a lot of money later if you get sick.

This second option covers eight of the most life threatening illnesses, including neurological and kidney problems, burns, cancer, heart disease, and transplants. Here's the kicker, the deductible is $20,000, so that's a pretty hefty out of pocket expense if you have a major incident.   You are responsible for anything up to $20,000 and then also fully responsible if it is not on their list of eight covered illnesses.

With health insurance, I'm looking to cover something serious. I can handle the little things, it's the big things that worry me. In addition, I think the type of care often depends on the coverage we have. Let's take a look at a common situation that might take place with each of these options we are talking about:

Suppose you have trouble with your knee. In the first case, you probably will need to go to a primary care doctor, who will send you to a specialist. The specialist will likely order a battery of tests and then schedule another appointment to review them. If the specialist is a surgeon and can see a way to fix the problem surgically, that will be the suggestion.

As the physician looks at the results, the question of insurance is likely to come up. Depending on our answer, we may we may get slightly different responses:

With the first option, where we have ample coverage and a low deductible, the surgeon will not hesitate to recommend a costly surgical procedure, particularly knowing there is an insurance company to foot the bill. Oh and by the way, his fee will go a long way to pay Johnny's next tuition payment. But let's give the doctor the benefit of the doubt, supposing the surgery is needed and can be successful most of the time. We would be silly not to do the surgery, after all the insurance company is "paying" for it, right? Or are they?   When we make a claim to the insurance company, we are the ones that are actually paying. They are just giving us back money we, along with many others in the same group, have already paid.

Likely the surgeon will give us a series of tasks to perform, including seeing a cardiologist to make sure our ticker is running right and having a blood test to make sure we good to go for surgery. Within a relatively short period of time, we are likely to find ourselves being wheeled into surgery.

Now let's look at the second case, where we have a high initial cost for any medical procedures, and the illness we have may not be covered at all. If we really need the surgery, and assuming the surgeon his worth his salt, he will likely still recommend an operation; but here's where things might be a bit different. If we have a high out of pocket amount for the surgery, or no coverage at all, in addition to recommending the surgery, the doctor may offer other choices. He may encourage us to look into physical therapy, homeopathic medicine, acupuncture, or any one of many other alternatives available. We can thank him for his advice, pay our visit and be on our way.

We can explore other options, pay for whatever medical consultations or studies need to be done, looking for an alternative to surgery. If after trying all our other options, we still don't get relief; we may very well find ourselves going back to the specialist, to have the surgery done, and having to pay for it with our own money, but at least we will have tried other alternatives.

One last option would be to simply forego the

surgery and hobble around. In reality, this is often what happens in many parts of the world where people often have limited access to health care and little or no savings to fund a costly operation.

I'm not talking about a perfect world here where we live in some kind of magic bubble, pretending we will never get sick, or worse yet in a place where we don't pay for insurance because it's not convenient. I'm talking about a world where we do get sick from time to time, have to go to the doctor, and make decisions about what must be done.

When we buy insurance, the company is betting we will probably be okay over time, so why shouldn't we?

In the case of health insurance, there are two ways we can insure ourselves. The first way is to be very savvy with our investments, so that we have a large capital base to handle any event, regardless of how big it is. The second is to have a plan to make money if we need an expensive procedure.

Often we focus only on having money with regards to our financial ability to handle a health risk. Ask any millionaire how this worked out for them on their death bed. But there is another way. We can have a means to make money if we need it. This is closer to what happens in much of the world. If someone gets sick, they go to the doctor. If they can't get cured right away and it turns out to be a costly procedure, they find out how much money they need for the operation. Then they weigh the cost against the potential for success. If they want to live, or fix what's wrong, and the operation has a high success rate, people can get pretty creative in terms of making money. Others cannot even imagine having to come up with thousands of dollars for a costly intervention. The first group may find relief from their ailments, the second will probably not. It's a harsh world, but that's reality.

If you needed to make money to cover a major illness, would you be able to do it?

If you have a large capital base and also are very confident in your ability to make money, consider insuring yourself medically; if not transfer this risk to the insurance company.

b) Create Your Own Insurance Company

If you like to "keep score" and see how you are doing on insuring yourself, I will give you a simple method to keep track of your progress. This section is for those who really like numbers and enjoy seeing how their strategy is working.

I'm going to give an example of how to do this for a family where the gross household income is $50,000. We'll say that they are pretty bright people, so they increase their income by 10% per year. I'm also assuming they invest in themselves 10% of their income, as I suggest:

Date	Income (Increase 10% yearly)	Savings (10%)	Insurance Premiums Saved ($200 increase per year)	Claims
$2,020	$50,000	$5,000	$100	$0
$2,021	$55,000	$5,500	$300	-$500
$2,022	$60,500	$6,050	$500	$0
$2,023	$66,550	$6,655	$700	$0
$2,024	$73,205	$7,321	$900	$0
$2,025	$80,526	$8,053	$1,100	-$2,000
$2,026	$88,578	$8,858	$1,300	$0
$2,027	$97,436	$9,744	$1,500	$0
$2,028	$107,179	$10,718	$1,700	$0
$2,029	$117,897	$11,790	$1,900	-$5,000
$2,030	$129,687	$12,969	$2,100	$0
Totals	$926,558	$92,656	$12,100	-$7,500

Net Gain (Loss) For your Insurance Company $97,256

In this example, I assume also you are able to save $100 in the first year by insuring yourself with the strategies I suggest, and that you are able to save an additional $200 per year as your capital base builds and you are able to handle more risk. I figure in three "claims" against the your company. One in 2021 for a stolen cell phone, one in 2025 for a computer that crashes, and another in 2029 for a car repair.

Obviously this is just an example. Actual experience is likely to be much more complicated and involved. Nevertheless, whenever you are offered an insurance you decline, you can put that in the amount of savings you have. If you have a problem with the item the proposed insurance would have taken care of, then it's a claim against you.

Your savings and claims will have much to do with how much risk you are willing to take. If you are not willing to take much risk, your savings are probably going to be negligible. As you take on more risk and insure yourself on more items, your savings will be more, but you could also have higher claims. That's the real world. Sometimes we win and others we lose.

This exercise is simply to see if the plan is working for you. If it is not, stick to a more traditional route and insure whatever you are afraid of losing. Everyone's experience is different. This is simply a way to see your progress in black and white.

Most notable in this exercise is to realize that the greatest benefit does not come from insuring ourselves, but rather by investing in ourselves.

Am I simplifying things too much? Perhaps, but it is to make a point. You don't have to be a highly paid professional, making a six figure income in order to free yourself from the dependence on others. What you really need is discipline. With it, there is no doubt you will be successful in your endeavor without it, you will likely struggle financially. This tool of keeping track of your progress is an excellent way to quantify your results .

c) Evaluate Your Risk Periodically

I like to think we go through three basic stages of life:

1. We prepare for it

2. We live it

3. We enjoy it

While the duration of each stage is different for each of us, our basic needs in terms of insurance are similar as we go through each. When we are young and growing up, we don't even know insurance exists. We may hear the word from time to time, but really don't fathom what it's all about. Then as we enter the second phase of life and begin to make purchases, insurance is often either included as part of the package, or sold as a additional benefit. Suddenly we are forced to begin learning about it as we go along, yet are often unaware of all its benefits and its drawbacks.

Insurance is likely to play a very important role in your life, like it or not. It's there just about wherever we go. Early on in our second stage of life, we should be careful to take care of our family, protecting against our untimely death or if we become disabled. With the way health care seems to be going, health insurance will probably always be at least some part of your financial situation, though it is up to you how you manage it.

Instead of battling against insurance, we can make it our friend. Find a good general insurance agent who you like. There are lots of them around, and as a group, they tend to be pretty nice people. Let them take care of your home, health, life, and accident insurance needs. They too have a family to feed. Having a good insurance agent is always helpful. Obviously there are many options Online which are also very competitive. In some cases you might want to have a local insurance agent, who is helpful to assist you if you have a claim, in others you can shop for the best value on the Internet.

As your capital base becomes larger, you should

become more confident in handling larger "claims" to your insurance company. As you manage more of your own risk, your dependence on your trusty insurance agent is likely to diminish, but keep him or her around, as there may be certain coverages you can never completely eliminate.

Perhaps one of the biggest turning points in our insurance needs come as our children are educated and are prepared for life. As they head into their second stage of life, this often coincides with us heading into our third stage. At this time, our necessity for insurance generally diminishes.

While providing a life of leisure for your children may seem tempting, be careful how much you give them. If we give them too much, they don't learn to fend for themselves, and in this world, we need to be adaptable and resilient above all.

If you are debt-free and have enough money in the bank to be cremated or buried, shouldn't that be enough? Does leaving a lot of wealth for children to fight over make our life more meaningful or less? These aren't easy questions. I certainly don't have all the answers, but I do believe the best inheritance we can leave our children is to instill confidence in their ability to overcome difficulty. This is much more valuable than any amount of money we can possibly leave them in any kind of investment.

It seems to me our children's education should be similar to the story about giving a man a fish to feed him for a day, or teaching him how to fish so he can feed himself for a lifetime. We can't just teach them about fish, we need to teach them how to fish. It's not enough to have to have a college degree, you need to know how to convert it into money. Sometimes having a trade needed by many is much better for providing income quickly, than a boatload of knowledge which won't even buy a bag of fries at your favorite fast-food restaurant.

As long as our kids know how to fend for themselves, they can make their own way. If we can help financially, so be it, but let's also let them overcome some of their own struggles. If we are always there to bail them out, what will they do when we are gone?

In our third stage of life, I believe we should pretty much do whatever we want to do. Work, if that's what you want to do, but don't do it because you have no other choice. If you are smart and resist temptation from time to time in the second part of your life, the third part will be much more comfortable when you get there. By the time you get to this stage of life, you want to be able to do as you please. Maybe you decide to dedicate yourself to a hobby, or start a different career. Why not? We only go around once in life.

Being in our third stage of life doesn't mean we are unproductive, it just means that hopefully we can be as productive or unproductive as we want to be; and if someone doesn't like it, then that's their problem, but we need to be disciplined to get there.

Your insurance coverage should change as you go through different stages of life. From your first introduction to it, to using it as a strategic part of your overall strategy, and finally by getting rid of your need for it; adjust your coverage accordingly as different stages of life present different risks.

Appendix

Og Mandino

God, I thank you for this day. I know I have not accomplished as yet all you expect of me, and if that is your reason for bathing me in the fresh dew of another dawn. I am most grateful. I am prepared, at last, to make you proud of me.

For full text of Seeds of Success by Og Mandino, you can find them in his excellent book, Mission:Success (pp. 143-148). Random House Publishing Group. Kindle Edition.

Robert Frost

Two roads diverged in a yellow wood,

And sorry I could not travel both

And be one traveler, long I stood

And looked down one as far as I could

To where it bent in the undergrowth;

Then took the other, as just as fair,

And having perhaps the better claim,

Because it was grassy and wanted wear;

Though as for that the passing there

Had worn them really about the same,

And both that morning equally lay

In leaves no step had trodden black.

Oh, I kept the first for another day!

Yet knowing how way leads on to way,

I doubted if I should ever come back.

I shall be telling this with a sigh

Somewhere ages and ages hence:

Two roads diverged in a wood, and I—

I took the one less traveled by,

And that has made all the difference.

Frost, Robert. "The Road Not Taken." By Robert Frost : The Poetry Foundation. The Poetry Foundation, n.d. Web. 21 Mar. 2013. <http://www.poetryfoundation.org/poem/173536>.

Don Miguel Ruiz & Rob McBride

1. I will be kind in thought, word, and action

2. I will take nothing personally and I will flow with everything

3. I will confirm perceptions before jumping to conclusions

4. I will give my best effort and live without regret

5. I will learn from everything and awaken my senses

1 - 4. Ruiz, Miguel. The Four Agreements: A Practical Guide to Personal Freedom. San Rafael, Calif: Amber-Allen Pub, 1997.

5. McBride, Rob. "Guiding Lights", Lunar Letter, August, 2009.

William Shakespeare

Beware of entrance to a quarrel, but being in,

Bear 't that th' opposed may beware of thee.

Give every man thy ear but few thy voice.

Take each man's censure but reserve thy judgment.

Costly thy habit as thy purse can buy,

But not expressed in fancy—rich, not gaudy,

For the apparel oft proclaims the man.

...

Neither a borrower nor a lender be,

For loan oft loses both itself and friend,

And borrowing dulls the edge of husbandry.

This above all: to thine own self be true,

And it must follow, as the night the day,

Thou canst not then be false to any man.

Shakespeare, William. Hamlet, act I, scene iii, 1599.

Theodore Roosevelt

It is not the critic who counts; not the man who points out how the strong man stumbles, or where the doer of deeds could have done them better. The credit belongs to the man who is actually in the arena, whose face is marred by dust and sweat and blood; who strives valiantly; who errs, who comes short again and again, because there is no effort without error and shortcoming; but who does actually strive to do the deeds; who knows great enthusiasms, the great devotions; who spends himself in a worthy cause; who at the best knows in the end the triumph of high achievement, and who at the worst, if he fails, at least fails while daring greatly, so that his place shall never be with those cold and timid souls who neither know victory nor defeat.

Roosevelt, Theodore. "Citizenship In A Republic" delivered at the Sorbonne, in Paris, France on 23 April, 1910

Mario Benedetti

Every day is one less day

every night another night

our heart wonders what it's all about

if everything is so brief and light

every beach is another beach except

when it is overtaken by the sea

and the four seasons make no noise

in the corners of reality

all of the gods are a god of nothing

and left without eternity

and in the meantime the birds

fight with the air as they learn to fly

every death is the death of another

and we forget them so as not to cry

but also there are those who / in innocence/

and in bare feet cross over to the other side

every day is one less day

and every night another night

but as long as there are roses in sight

life is a celebration in which to delight

Benedetti, Mario. Existir Todavía, "Más o Menos", 2003 (rhm).

Joan Manuel Serrat

Everything stays and everything goes,

but ours is to go,

to go making roads,

roads over the ocean.

I never went after glory,

nor to leave on the minds
of men my song;
I love the simple things,
weightless and light,
like soap bubbles.

I like to watch as they
reflect the sun and the grain.
fly under the great blue sky,
suddenly shake and then break.

I never went after glory...

Walking is the road, your footsteps,
and nothing more;
walking, there is no road,
the road is made as you go.

As you go you make your road
and as you look back you see
the road over which you
will never again go.
Walking there is no road
only the wake you leave
as you go...

For a very long time and in that very same place

the forests have been dressed with thorns.

A poet was heard shouting:

"Walking there is no road,

we make our road as we go..."

blow by blow, verse by verse

The poet died a long way from home.

The dust of a neighboring nation

covers his soul.

As he left they saw him cry:

"Walking there is no road,

we make our road as we go..."

blow by blow, verse by verse

When the songbird no longer sings,

when the poet is a pilgrim,

when not even praying helps:

"Walking there is no road,

we make our road as we go..."

blow by blow, verse by verse...

blow by blow, verse by verse...

blow by blow, verse by verse.

Serrat, Joan Manuel & Machado, discography Antonio, Zafiro/Novola, 1969 (rhm).

Mario Benedetti

Make it a great day... unless, of course, you have other plans.

This morning I woke up excited about all of the things I have to do today before the alarm went off.

I have responsibilities to fulfill. I am important. My job today is to determine what kind of day I will have.

Today I can complain because it's raining... or I can give thanks because the plants are being watered.

Today I can feel sad because I don't have more money... or I can be happy because my financial situation drives me to plan my purchases more carefully.

Today I can complain about my health... or rejoice I am alive.

Today I can lament all my parents didn't give me while I was growing up... or I can be grateful that because of them I am here now.

Today I can cry because the roses have thorns... or I can celebrate the thorns have roses.

Today I can feel sorry for myself because I don't have many friends... or I can get excited and embark on an adventure to find new relationships.

Today I can complain because I have to go to work... or I can shout with joy because I have a job.

Today I can complain because I have to go to school... or I can open my mind energetically and fill it with new and rich knowledge.

Today I can mumble bitterly because I have housework to do... or I can feel honored because I have a roof for my mind and my body.

Today the day presents itself before me waiting for me to give it form, and here I am, I am the sculptor.

What happens today, depends on me. I choose what kind of day I am going to have today.

Make it a great day... unless, of course, you have other plans.

Mario Benedetti (rhm), source unknown. There is some doubt as to the authorship of this passage.

Facundo Cabral

Your not depressed, you're distracted. Distracted by the life which fills you. You have a heart, a brain, a soul and a spirit, so how can you feel poor and wretched. Distracted by the life which surrounds you, dolphins, forests, oceans, mountains, and rivers.

Don't fall into what your brother fell who suffers for one human being when there are more than 5.6 billion in the world and besides, it's not so bad living alone. I enjoy each moment deciding what I am going to do and thanks to the solitude, I know myself which is fundamental for living. Don't fall into what your father fell, who feels old at 70, forgetting that Moses led the exodus at 80 and Rubinstein played Chopin like nobody at 90, just to cite two known examples.

You're not depressed, your distracted. You think you lost something, which is impossible because everything has been given to you. You didn't make even one single strand of hair on your head, as such you can't own anything, and besides life doesn't take things from you, it frees you from them, making you lighter so you can fly higher and reach plenitude. From the cradle to the coffin is a university and that is why what you think are problems are actually lessons, and life is dynamic, and why it is in constant movement. As such, you need only be aware of the present.

You didn't lose anyone, those who have died simply beat you to the punch, because we are all headed there. Besides, the best of them, their love, continues in your heart...

You can't find happiness and it's so easy. You need only listen first to your heart before your head intervenes...

Do only what you love and you will be happy because those who do what they love are blessedly condemned to success, which must come when it should come, because what must be, will be and will come naturally. Don't do anything out of obligation or commitment, rather for love. Then there will be plenitude and in this plenitude everything is possible, without force, because the natural force of life moves you.

Facundo Cabral (rhm)

Rob McBride

Life is made up of moments...

Moments which make us quiver with emotion and form an integral part of existence. Moments which become the motion picture of our life and can be replayed 24/7 to anchor us in those experiences that confirm how marvelous it is to be on this incredible journey we call life.

Moments from day to day which comprise a surprising number of our minutes, ours and days. Minutes which can be overlooked if we are not paying attention: the flight of a bird, the intense color of a flower, the invisible air that gives us life.

McBride, Rob. Magic Moments (2008).

Louis Armstrong

I see trees of green, red roses too

I see them bloom for me and you

And I think to myself

What a wonderful world

I see skies of blue and clouds of white

The bright blessed day, the dark sacred night

And I think to myself

What a wonderful world

The colors of the rainbow, so pretty in the sky

Are also on the faces of people goin' by

I see friends shakin' hands, sayin'

"How do you do?"

They're really sayin',

"I love you."

I hear babies cry, I watch them grow

They'll learn much more than I'll ever know

And I think to myself

What a wonderful world

Yes, I think to myself

What a wonderful world

Songwriter: Doug Dipreta

Glossary of Terms

ANNUITY - An insurance product providing a lifetime payment of a certain amount of money at a certain age.

BOND - An obligation by a company or a central government paying a specific rate of interest for a specified period of time

COMMISSION - The amount of money paid by the insurance company to its salespeople

DEATH BENEFIT - The amount of money paid to beneficiaries by an insurance company upon death of an insured person

DEDUCTIBLE - The amount of money we pay on a claim before the insurance company pays.

DOLLAR COST AVERAGING - Investing a similar amount of money into an investment as its price rises and falls

INDEX FUNDS - A basket of investments mirroring a particular index in the capital markets

MUTUAL FUNDS - Professionally managed asset

pools of funds investing in a wide variety of financial instruments

MORTALITY COST - The amount an insurance company charges to cover a death benefit

PAID-UP POLICY - The point when no further premiums are required to keep a life insurance policy in force.

PREMIUM - The amount of money an insurance company charges to insure against the occurrence of a particular risk for a certain amount of time

STOCK - An instrument whereby you own a small fraction of a company

TERM LIFE INSURANCE - An insurance contract whereby the company promises to pay a death benefit if you die within the time period stated in the policy

UNIVERSAL LIFE INSURANCE - An insurance contract whereby the company promises to pay a death benefit if you die while the policy is in force and also offers and investment side of the contract which can be invested in different options

VOLATILITY - When the value of an investment goes up or down to due market factors

WHOLE LIFE INSURANCE - An insurance contract whereby the insurance company promises to pay a death benefit when you die, as long as premiums are being paid, or the policy is paid-up

About This Book

I got married at 23, and shortly afterward I was introduced to insurance. While I have had different coverages, for different reasons over time, there is one insurance coverage I never thought twice about renewing: Health Insurance.

Over the years, I've pretty much done as I suggest in this manual. I stopped buying extended service warranties, began insuring myself on my vehicles and other items, but never stopped paying for health insurance.

A few days before my coverage lapsed in March of this year, I decided to change from a local policy in Venezuela where I live, to an international policy giving broader coverage. In spite of filling out the application for the new insurance and sending it in before the end of the grace period on my original insurance, the process has taken a little longer than I expected.

On April 1st I woke up without insurance for the first time in my life in over 30 years. It was a strange feeling, I somehow felt naked in the world; yet at the same time, it made me begin to think about the whole idea behind insurance. Specifically my thoughts revolved around whether or not I could handle this last risk, which I had not yet been willing to insure myself.

Through a lack of foresight on my part, I was caught with my pants down, suddenly I had no insurance, in a world where I had just automatically assumed that health insurance, was always needed.

I'm a big numbers guy. On the 1st, 2nd, and 3rd days of the 4th month of this year I was in deep thought regarding my health insurance. On the third day I woke up at 4:44 AM, ready to rock and roll, pumped with the idea about "Insuring Yourself." The more I thought about the situation, the more I became convinced I could handle the risk, not necessarily with the capital base I currently have, but with my ability to make money if I need it.

That same morning, I began writing this book you now have in your hands. As I wrote, I realized two things. The first is that more than just giving you a way to "insure yourself," my true hope is that you "free yourself." Being able to save money on insurance is really just a by-product of being able to be truly free.

I hate paying insurance, as do many people. This is the catch and why people might find this book interesting. We see insurance as a necessary evil, and often it is. There are certain times we can assume a risk and others when we cannot. We also have to be realistic.

The other thing I realized along the way is that I am not yet ready to insure myself completely. The health insurance element is too big to leave uncovered. So as I write these words, I have my application in place to be covered against most of the major medical problems that can happen to us, with a deductible which will sting pretty bad if I have to use it, but could save me financially if I do.

It's not a perfect world. Finding balance and equilibrium isn't easy. We have constant pressures pushing us in different directions, making sense of it isn't easy.

Within the next several days after my revelation about "Insure Yourself Today," I had written the backbone of this short manual. What you have before you is what 34 years of life have taught me for better or worse. Some of the lessons have been more difficult to learn than others, but they have all been valuable.

Surely you will face your own difficulties. I don't propose this plan will help you avoid problems. On the contrary, I'm pretty sure you will have some along the way, but my sincere hope is that these words help you to be able to inspire yourself, if you find yourself getting off track.

While each element in this book is important to being free, perhaps inspiring yourself is the most important. If we know how to get back up, after we are down, we have a powerful way to continue on despite difficulty. Make no doubt about it, your shares of troubles will come, it's a part of life. Ironically, as time goes on, our troubles tend to be the most memorable of moments.

My dilemma regarding insurance is what drove me to write this book, but I now realize its scope is much broader. My aim is give you a tool providing you with the ability to free yourself from the chains which might otherwise hold you down.

Break free and live the life you have always dreamed of living!

www.ingramcontent.com/pod-product-compliance
Lightning Source LLC
Chambersburg PA
CBHW030810180526
45163CB00003B/1226